Donald Kiraly & Sarah Signer
Scaffolded Language Emergence in the Classroom

Sprachen lehren – Sprachen lernen
Herausgegeben von Peggy Katelhön und Martina Nied Curcio
Band 4

Donald Kiraly & Sarah Signer

Scaffolded Language Emergence in the Classroom

From Theory to Practice

Verlag für wissenschaftliche Literatur

Cover: "Hyde Park Denizen", photograph created by Corey Phillips Fowler
(http://cpfowlerphotography.squarespace.com/)

ISBN 978-3-7329-0259-0
ISBN (E-Book) 978-3-7329-9677-3
ISSN 2364-7116

© Frank & Timme GmbH Verlag für wissenschaftliche Literatur
Berlin 2017. Alle Rechte vorbehalten.

Das Werk einschließlich aller Teile ist urheberrechtlich geschützt.
Jede Verwertung außerhalb der engen Grenzen des Urheberrechts-
gesetzes ist ohne Zustimmung des Verlags unzulässig und strafbar.
Das gilt insbesondere für Vervielfältigungen, Übersetzungen,
Mikroverfilmungen und die Einspeicherung und Verarbeitung in
elektronischen Systemen.

Herstellung durch Frank & Timme GmbH,
Wittelsbacherstraße 27a, 10707 Berlin.
Printed in Germany.
Gedruckt auf säurefreiem, alterungsbeständigem Papier.

www.frank-timme.de

Contents

Acknowledgements 7

Don Kiraly

SECTION I: THE GENESIS AND THEORETICAL UNDERPINNINGS OF THE SLE APPROACH

Introducing *Scaffolded Language Emergence* –
An approach but not a method 11

Chapter 1: SLE – A post-method approach for
initiating foreign language emergence 14

Chapter 2: Initial steps towards the SLE approach 24

Chapter 3: *Structuro-Global Audio-Visual (SGAV)* methodology:
a partially successful attempt to shift from an instructionist
to a constructivist epistemology 29

Chapter 4: The *Natural Approach*: comprehensible input
and a cognitivist epistemology 39

Chapter 5: A case for emergence as the key process
underlying language learning 48

Chapter 6: Pedagogical beacons 60

SARAH SIGNER

SECTION II: FROM THEORY TO EXEMPLARY PRACTICE

Introduction 77

Chapter 7: Affordances, signifiers and embodiment in the SLE classroom 78

Chapter 8: Teaching-centred vs autonomous learning 85

Chapter 9: Autonomy and collaboration in the SLE classroom 92

Chapter 10: Material affordances and the learning environment 103

Chapter 11: Beyond teaching – From scaffolding to emergence 111

DON KIRALY

SECTION III: A PROLOGUE… INSTEAD OF A CONCLUSION

Chapter 12: Initial guidelines for Scaffolded Language Emergence
facilitators 127

References 136

Acknowledgements

As the approach to foreign language emergence outlined in this book evolved from my very first experiences as a language teacher in the 1970s in Lyons, France, I would like to express my gratitude to Carol Bausor and my good friend Debora Prichard-Clément, who introduced me to the *All's Well* method back then. Despite the fact that I was an absolute newcomer to the language teaching profession at the time, they set the stage, with their profound understanding of the potential of *SGAV* methodology and particularly its humanistic, post-positivist and holistic qualities for bringing real change – and joy – to the language learning classroom.

To my favourite professors in the field of foreign language education at the University of Illinois at Champaign-Urbana in the 1980s: Sandra Savignon, Jim Lee and Bill Van Patten, I owe my heartfelt thanks for introducing me to the *Natural Approach* and *Communicative Language Teaching* and for being exceptional mentors and role models.

My appreciation also goes out to the many student-facilitators at the University of Mainz who have contributed to the development of the SLE approach by creating and running courses based on this approach in 13 languages over the past ten years. I am also grateful to the students who participated in my seminar on language emergence in the winter semester of 2016–17 and who provided invaluable feedback from a student's perspective on my section of the book. They are (in no particular order):

Beatrice Lipani	Luca Matthies	Pauline Meurer
Claire Bocklet	Francesca Fritella	Brenda Finocchiaro
Johanna Greenslade	Lisa Immerheiser	Katharina Lautermilch
Khrystyna Oliynyk	Irina Pohl	Narindra Razakarivelo
Lena Sümenicht	Janine Theimert	Lara Wältner
Manuel Riveros	Selina Oechsler	Dawid Suferowicz
Paloma Abad Villar	Daniel Ballestin	Jael Schilling
Phillip Wolf	Blanka Jagodzinska	Yvonne Scheuerling
Sebastian Fobbe	Jana Gawalleck	Wiktoria Nowogrodzka
Yvonne Najduch		

The authors of the excellent theses that served as the basis for Section II of this book deserve a special word of thanks as well. Without their interest in SLE and their first-rate academic work, we would not have the wealth of qualitative data that provided Sarah with concrete examples of SLE at work. The authors (in alphabetical order are:

Marie Buring
Joeri Destreel
Sabina Heinrichsohn
Jennifer Nagi
Alessia Rizzo
Stefanie Scheu
Annika Wittner

Kate Garrett's first-rate editing and proofreading of the entire manuscript and her insightful constructive criticisms contributed enormously to the final product.

I would like to also thank my cousin Corey Phillips Fowler for the gift of the magnificent photograph that graces the cover of the book. This image reflects the essence of what this volume is about.

Penultimately, I would like to thank those colleagues of mine at the University of Mainz that contributed their time, energy, insights and moral support at various stages of the SLE development process. In particular, my profound thanks go out to Prof. Andreas Kelletat, who was responsible for the School's Language Centre during the 'B1 in nine months project', Prof. Silvia Hansen-Schirra, the head of my department, who has been an indefatigable source of inspiration and support, and Dr. Thomas Kempa and Tobias Briest, both of whom have directed the School's language centre in recent years, and both of whom have tirelessly supported my efforts to continue the work on developing SLE ever since the 'B1 in nine months' project ended.

And finally, I wish to thank my wife, Christa Noll-Kiraly, who has been a perpetually insightful interlocutor and an eminently patient listener over the past eight months while my section of this book emerged.

All of these individuals as well as the scores of FTSK students who have participated enthusiastically and successfully in SLE courses over the past ten years deserve my profound appreciation. But I am of course solely responsible for any flaws or errors my text may contain.

Don Kiraly

Don Kiraly

SECTION I: THE GENESIS AND THEORETICAL UNDERPINNINGS OF THE SLE APPROACH

Introducing *Scaffolded Language Emergence* – An approach but not a method

The history of language teaching is a history dominated by one particular approach that dates back at least hundreds of years if not millennia and that has been used virtually the world over to impart knowledge of learners' non-native languages. Back in 1987, William E. Rutherford, an eminent scholar in second language acquisition and foreign language teaching, wrote:

> […] a glimpse at the methodological history of language teaching is very instructive, for it reveals that for centuries on end […] there was essentially one way to teach languages – one that extends into the present – and that is what is known as grammar-translation. (Rutherford 1987: 209)

And 20 years later, Dalke et al. (2007) formulated their view on the near-monolithic state of language teaching as follows:

> Despite all the work done in progressive education, many teachers continue to imagine, and are often encouraged to believe, that the most effective and efficient method involves a structured environment, in which the instructor imparts carefully packaged information to students, to digest and incorporate into their existing knowledge base. (Dalke et al. 2007: 111)

And yet, alternative approaches to the 'packaged information' paradigm in foreign language teaching have been legion. Most of them have been met with some, and in a few cases – like Steven Krashen's *Natural Approach* – considerable initial acceptance and success. But virtually all of them have ultimately fallen by the wayside, leaving in place what I believe is still the highly transmissionist practice of attempting to transfer bits and pieces of knowledge about a language to would-be learners (despite the lip service paid in recent decades to 'communication' in the foreign language classroom). Some of the alternative approaches of recent decades appear to be on rather dubious theoretical footing which may have precipitated their demise: an enormous amount of criticism has been aimed at the *Natural Approach*, for instance, due to the alleged lack of evidence for and the unfalsifiability of Krashen's renowned five hypotheses. (see, for example: Taylor: 2004, Gregg: 1984, Liu: 2015, McGlaughlin: 1978). [1]

This little book aims to share with readers interested in promising alternatives to conventional foreign language teaching some of the steps along a journey. This is a journey that I have undertaken in collaboration with many colleagues and students towards developing an approach that I believe could be feasible for certain kinds of learners, but that has so far not been subjected to rigorous empirical research. This book could be a first step towards undertaking such research. Let it be noted at the outset: *Scaffolded Language Emergence* (SLE) is to be understood as an approach ([which I define, borrowing loosely from Richards and Rogers (1986)] as a tapestry of interwoven assumptions and learning design features deduced from those assumptions), rather than a method (a detailed, session-by-session roadmap for instruction – typically based on an approach). I have included no ready-made lesson plans, cookie-cutter exercises, or lists of vocabulary or grammatical structures that are to be taught or learned because to do so would have meant contradicting the very essence of this approach. (The book does, however, contain a selection of scenes and techniques from various courses created and run on the basis of the principles presented in this volume).

The book is divided into two main sections:

1. A review of the key experiences and epiphanies that led to the development of this approach. This section deals with both the genesis and the theoretical framework of the SLE approach and how communicative competence can be understood and dealt with as an emergent (non-linear, dynamic and autopoietic) system; and
2. From theory to practice: examples of the principles at work, beneficial outcomes and caveats for would-be SLE facilitators.

---

1 In order to skirt criticisms of non-falsifiability, I have intentionally avoided proposing any hypotheses like those upon which Steven Krashen's Natural Approach (Krashen 1982, Krashen & Terrell 1983) was based regarding the nature of language learning processes. Instead, I have drawn on what I see as a set of abductive assumptions that reflect my pragmatistic, social constructivist and post-positivist epistemology. It has not been my objective to discover how language acquisition actually occurs in the real world, but instead to propose a plausible set of assumptions and a course of action for initiating and stimulating Ln communicative competence in adults.

Section I: The initial section outlines and elucidates the theoretical foundations and practical genesis of the SLE approach. The chapters in this section will 1) discuss my own experience with various language teaching methods dating back as far as 1977, including: [*Structuro-global Audio-Visual (SGAV)*] methodology developed in France in the 1960s and 1970s, Krashen and Terrell's *Natural Approach* and *Total Physical Response*, 2) the implications of a social constructivist epistemology for Ln development; and 3) language learning seen as an *emergent* process: the especial relevance of complexity thinking and language ecology in foreign language education, which has been a major focus of the ground-breaking research conducted by a number of language education scholars including: Leo Van Lier (1996, 2000, 2005), Diane Larsen-Freeman (1997, 2007, 2011), and Nick Ellis (1998).

Section II: The second section of this volume was written by my colleague Sarah Signer, a trained translator who is also a regular teaching staff member at the FTSK of the University of Mainz. Sarah has a CELTA qualification in Teaching English as a Foreign Language. She worked for a year full-time as a TEFL teacher in China and has spent five additional years teaching English part-time at various institutions in Germany. However, she has never actually taught or participated in an SLE course. Hence, she epitomises an important target group I wish to address with this book: trained and experienced teachers who are interested in looking beyond conventional instructional approaches to language teaching. In the second section of the book, Sarah discusses a cornucopia of practical examples illustrating the special nature of SLE courses – all offered at the FTSK over the last ten years. These examples are all drawn from BA and MA theses written by students under my supervision at the FTSK in recent years.

Section III: This brief concluding section, written by Don Kiraly, summarises the key features of SLE courses in the form of some basic initial guidelines to help would-be SLE facilitators create and run their own foreign language courses.

Chapter 1: SLE – A post-method approach for initiating foreign language emergence

This volume lays out the foundation of my approach as an invitation to current and prospective language teachers to use in the creation of their own courses and 'facilitated learning' materials and particularly activities. The claim was made in the field of foreign language teaching some time ago that we are now in the "post-method" stage of its evolution (Karavamakulu: 2003), and I do not intend to contradict that characterisation here. Dozens of SLE courses (most of them short and intensive) in many languages have been taught at my home institution, the University of Mainz, Germany, over the past ten years – all of them crafted largely from scratch by small teams of relatively untrained language teachers on the basis of the SLE approach. In other words, all of our teacher-facilitators have simultaneously been the designers of the courses they have gone on to offer.

Provided with an introduction to the theoretical foundation of assumptions and design principles, as well as extensive scaffolding on my part during the planning stage, these novice teachers in essence have all created their own language courses. As a result each course has been unique, but also dependent on the course design and facilitating capabilities of each team of teacher facilitators (and also adapted to the myriad features of each group of learners). The spirit and practice of the SLE-based classes we have run over the years at the FTSK, in my view, are completely in tune with those of the Dogme post-method approach developed by Luke Meddings and Scott Thornbury (2003, 2009) – which I only discovered late in the process of writing this volume on SLE. In explaining what makes the Dogme mindset (which they prefer to call it instead of a method or approach) different from that underlying conventional instruction, Meddings and Thornbury state:

> A dogme lesson can feel like a group of people freed from their expectations of the traditional teacher-student, them-and-us, relationship: a group of people enjoying the freedom of using language to talk about immediate, real concerns; a group of people reassured by the teacher's interest in them, in their experience, and – critically – in **their** language use and needs. (Authors' emphasis) (2003: 1)

The guide to the Dogme approach for teachers (Meddings and Thornbury 2009) provides a perspective on the theoretical underpinnings of the mindset that is somewhat different yet – in my view – completely compatible with that underlying SLE, and it also includes a wealth of sample activities that could be used in virtually any humanistic, post-method classroom. The present volume specifically avoids including a section with such sample recommended activities because every single one included in Meddings and Thornbury's *Teaching Unplugged* (2009) would fit perfectly in an SLE classroom – if the learners had the requisite communicative skills to undertake those activities. Unlike Dogme, however, SLE is aimed specifically at real or recent newcomers to a language, that is, at learners who do not have more than the most rudimentary foreign language tools and skills at their disposal. The Dogme approach revolves around conversation (rather than drills, exercises, textbooks or other contrived learning materials), but SLE is designed for beginning students who cannot yet converse in the foreign language. It is clear that there will be plenty of room in SLE courses for the very same kind of student-focused conversation as proposed in the Dogme approach. But in my view, it is essential to provide far more scaffolding for learners' early emergent language as they enter and move beyond the basic elementary stage in order to ensure that they will have the necessary basic communicative tools to pursue learning in a variety of ways and venues – including conversational settings. In my view, the Dogme approach would be an ideal way to structure a language emergence environment once a basic level of communicative competence has been achieved – for example, within an SLE-based course.

It will become clear throughout this volume that SLE facilitators initially spend a great deal of time and effort creating activities in which learning can occur – and scaffolding that learning. Nevertheless, the underlying idea of setting the stage for learning opportunities that will be modified and expanded through the participation of the learners is summed up succinctly by Meddings and Thornbury in their presentation of the Dogme approach.

> Rather than preparing lessons, and marching students down the road laid out in advance, the dogme teacher is prepared for a lesson that is co-authored by the people in the room (ibid.)

This concept of co-authorship is primordial in the SLE approach as well. As those readers who might consider themselves to be conventional language teachers working with a textbook-based method will already have surmised, the commitment of SLE teachers in terms of time and energy (at least while they are preparing their very first SLE course) is likely to be considerable. They have no textbooks to take off the shelf, no ready-made tasks, activities or exercises to draw on, and no pre-selected texts with pre-formulated questions to discuss in class. Instead, the onus is on them to interpret the tapestry of the approach, create activities that can serve as opportunities for language emergence, and then facilitate and scaffold the learners' participation in those activities. At this point, I would like to set the Dogme conversational approach aside and focus specifically on the origin of the SLE approach with its emphasis on beginning or very elementary learners, keeping in mind that, in my view, the SLE mindset and the Dogme mindset are almost identical: SLE is designed for beginners and Dogme is suited for more advanced learners.

Do we still need alternative approaches to language learning?

Before moving on to the genesis and principles underlying the SLE approach, I would like to briefly introduce the critical view of mainstream scholastic language teaching that was outlined by Werner Bleyhl (2005), a professor of English Language and Literature at the Ludwigsburg University of Education in Germany. That article was published at about the same time that I began to actively develop the SLE approach to foreign language teaching that this volume introduces. As a prominent professor, teacher trainer and pedagogical researcher working within the field of foreign language education, Bleyhl was responsible for training foreign language teachers at a German university – hardly an iconoclast with some shiny new pedagogical gimmick to sell. I believe it is worth taking a quick look at Bleyhl's critique of conventional language teaching methodologies, which he saw as being still largely dominated by an outdated Cartesian understanding of the nature of learning. This understanding includes three key tenets: the validity of reductionism, the duality of mind and body, and the primacy of conscious awareness over holistic, embodied enaction in the pedagogical domain. Bleyhl criticises all three tenets for not being in tune with recent findings in various fields of inquiry. The Cartesian worldview, Bleyhl argues, imposes a pervasively and perniciously reductionist focus on the linearly organised, rote learning of language structures as standard fare in language classroom activities. [2]

From this perspective, in conventional approaches to language teaching, the situated, embodied and experiential nature of language use is frequently given rather short shrift to the detriment of whole-person and interpersonal learning (as well as students' motivation). Even the 'communicative' approaches, which have been so much in vogue since the 1990s, Bleyhl sees as often being subverted by a contrived pseudo-situationality that learners perceive as dubious. Rather than supporting learners in a naturally self-organising process as they should, teachers, Bleyhl claims, are often overly concerned with controlling the largely uncontrollable and unpredictable self-organising process of language acquisition (2005: 18). Bleyhl rejects the rationalist epistemology of conventional instructionist practice reflected in the view of the teacher as a distributor of knowledge. He also rejects the Platonic and Chomskyan conceptualisations of the innate nature of universal grammar [interestingly, this conceptualisation appears to have also been adopted by Krashen (Liu: 2015: 159)].

In Bleyhl's view, cognitivist (rule-based, computer-like) portrayals of the nature of language use and development persist up to the present day as part of the theoretical foundations of a plethora of language-teaching methods. Bleyhl's emphasis on the self-organising nature of learning reflects the view of language development as an emergent process that already dates back at least two decades (Larsen-Freeman: 1997). Building on the view of conventional language teaching depicted by Bleyhl, the Scaffolded Language Emergence approach seeks to offer teachers and learners an alternative view of language learning processes and objectives that can help them see language learning in a radically different light. Instead of considering second language development to be deductive in nature, linear, reductionist and rule-governed, SLE embraces a holistic and eminently social understanding of language learning. The key assumption is that, for a language to emerge (i.e. to develop autopoietically[3]), it

---

2   For invaluable discussions on the post-positivist critique of Cartesian education, the reader might like to consider the work of visionary scholars like William Doll (1993), and Brent Davis and Dennis Sumara (2006, 2008, 2010). These scholars, none of whom is a specialist in foreign language education, have been absolutely inspirational in furthering my own search to understand the nature of learning and how to promote it in foreign language education and translator education.

3   The term autopoietic, meaning "self-creating" in ancient Greek, was introduced by Varela et al. (1974) to describe the self-maintaining chemistry of living cells. It is now being used to refer to similar features in a wide range of systems in various fields.

must do so through actual use in authentic acts of communication and not merely or primarily in tasks contrived and closely controlled by textbook authors and classroom teachers.

Perhaps the most salient difference between Bleyhl's task-based learning perspective and the SLE approach is that he explicitly subscribes to a radical constructivist epistemology (based on Piaget's theory of cognitive development). SLE, however, depends on a social constructivist understanding of learning (based largely on the socio-cultural learning theory of Lev Vygotsky) and on complexity thinking (which will be discussed in Chapter 5), which is completely absent from Bleyhl's writings. In my view, this is an important distinction, but one that does not by any means vitiate my agreement with Bleyhl's critique of conventional teaching approaches.

In a nutshell, Piaget's (and by extension, Bleyhl's) view emphasises that the construction of meaning and knowledge occurs largely in intra-cranial space, that is, essentially as a localised cognitive process within the brain, mind and skull of each learner. Vygotsky (1994), by contrast, insisted that meaning and knowledge are co-constructed through social interaction. Hence, for Bleyhl, the knowledge gleaned by completing tasks in task-based learning approaches primarily reflects comprehension reached through each individual's personal cognitive and physical interactions with actual objects and events in that person's environment. I, however, find myself epistemologically leaning towards Vygotsky's theory of learning as also – and in fact most fundamentally – related to the socially mediated and negotiated meanings of shared experiences in the physical, social and cultural worlds in which learners are embedded and embodied.

The goals of this volume

The primary objective of this book is to introduce SLE as a principled approach to fostering initial language emergence in adults. It is both firmly grounded in extensive experience and supported by a growing body of theory that sees language learning as an emergent, highly authentic and collaborative process of language creation rather than one of receiving and then applying carefully-packaged linguistic rules and structures. The Scaffolded Language Emergence approach has deep roots in three domains: 1) naturalistic, immersion-type language learning as exemplified in a long lineage of language teaching methods, 2) the body of general educational thought revolving around the concept of social constructivism, which dates back at least to early 20th century progressive thinkers like Lev Vygotsky and John Dewey, and 3) the school of thought in the domain of language learning and acquisition studies that focuses on the ecology and complexity of language and both social and cognitive language learning processes. As stated at the outset, the SLE approach – at this point – is not directly based on the results of a significant body of empirical research. Rather than being derived from the inductive collection of data or the deduction of suitable didactic practices from a set of unfalsifiable rules or laws, it should instead be seen in terms of an interwoven network of assumptions derived abductively. As the assumptions and design principles comprising the approach are now finally being formulated extensively for publication in this volume, and as the approach has been used successfully to help many hundreds of students to acquire elementary communicative competence in one of many languages to date, this initiatory guide is also intended as an invitation to language teaching researchers to undertake empirical research to test the approach and the validity of its assumptions.

The essence of the approach in a nutshell

From an SLE perspective, and as mentioned above, conventional approaches to language teaching often purport to offer learners carefully packaged information about language to be accumulated through deduction from linguistic rules, rote memorisation and repetitive practice. SLE, on the other hand, advocates the creation of a naturalistic immersion environment in which adult learners in particular can explore and in fact generate within themselves a previously unknown language system through collaboration with peers and with one or more *facilitators* who nudge, guide and scaffold far more than they instruct. Readers who are familiar with some of the common 'alternative' approaches to foreign language learning (like the *Silent Way*, the *Natural Approach*, the *Whole Language Movement*, *Community Language Learning* or *Suggestopedia*[4]) as well as less radical successors to the classic *Grammar-Translation method*, which was originally designed to teach Latin and ancient Greek, are likely to find that certain techniques used in courses designed on

---

4   See Earl Stevick's classic work on alternative approaches to language teaching (1980). Stevick also outlines the *Grammar-Translation method*.

the basis of various 'alternative' approaches are similar – at least superficially – to some of those developed for SLE sessions.

And it is likely that many of the specific activities used in SLE courses will appear familiar to experienced conventional language teachers, particularly ones who attempt to regularly incorporate authentic interaction and ludic moments in their classroom activities. SLE does not claim to offer any magic bullets to generate communicative competence effortlessly and within a brief period of time. What makes it unique, I believe, is instead the specific constellation of pedagogical epistemology, learning theory and praxis that comprise the approach – as well as its specific objective of encouraging language emergence at the earliest possible stage (that is, before resorting to the study of rules).

This co-authored volume represents the first (albeit very modest) book-length publication on SLE, which I have developed over the past decade at the *Fachbereich Translation, Sprach- und Kulturwissenschaft* – FTSK (school of translation, linguistics and cultural studies) of the University of Mainz, Germany. Rather than purporting to be a way to *teach* a foreign language, the SLE approach is aimed at providing scaffolded but dynamic and frequently collaborative classroom-based opportunities for adults to bootstrap themselves into incipient communicative competence in virtually any foreign language.

This book is intended as an initiatory handbook for language teachers and teachers-in-training who are interested in learning how one might facilitate naturalistic language development rather than (or at least in addition to) merely improving the contents or delivery of *instruction* (which here is used to refer to the conventional direct transmission of knowledge and skills from teachers to learners). With the help of numerous students and colleagues, I have created the SLE approach first in the Division of American Studies and subsequently in the Division of English Linguistics and Translation Studies of the FTSK – one of the oldest and largest translator and interpreter education institutions in Europe. But in fact, the approach has deeper practical roots that extend back to my pedagogical experiences at the very beginning of my 40 years of professional involvement with and study of various language teaching approaches and methods. Those approaches and methods include the second generation *Structuro-Global Audio-Visual* (*SGAV*) methods developed in the 1970s at the *Centre de recherche et d'étude pour la diffusion du français* (Crédif) in France, Steven Krashen and Tracy Terrell's *Natural Approach* and James Asher's *Total Physical Response*, as well as the *Notional-Functional Approach* and the *Communicative Approach* that appeared in the 1980s.

Within the scope of the SLE approach that my students, colleagues and I have developed and applied at the FTSK, perhaps the most fundamental of the few core principles behind it is strict adherence to the principle of 'second-language only' interaction in the elementary language classroom (that is, for about the first 50–75 hours of learning sessions). This feature of the approach was initially borrowed from both the *Natural Approach* and *SGAV* methodology, but it has proven to be one of the keys to the success of the many SLE courses we have offered in a number of languages at the FTSK. We have consistently found that when the use of the students' native tongue is off-limits in the classroom, students will communicate first through body language and then gradually through the ever-increasing (and increasingly complex) use of the developing Ln itself. In this way, the second language can emerge – with little overt interference from the students' native language. Language emergence is seen as the natural result of both the inborn desire of human beings to communicate and the autopoietic nature of (communicative) language competence.

The teacher's (or rather the facilitator's[5]) responsibilities in an SLE classroom include assuming a key role (in collaboration with the learners) in creating a physical, social and cultural environment in which learners bootstrap themselves into a position of being able to communicate via the second language. Instead of instructional classroom exercises where teachers attempt to 'teach' features of the language and where learners might be expected to parrot, ingest, practice and regurgitate what they are being taught, SLE emergence activities involve iterative (rather than repetitive), scaffolded and authenticated[6] social interaction that sets the stage for the naturalistic development of the second language as the group's lingua franca and as an autopoietic system within each course participant.

Whenever possible, facilitators work in pairs or small teams to initiate, plan and run SLE courses at the FTSK. Ideally, these courses are offered in an intensive format (at least 25 hours per week) by at least two native (or near-native) speaker facilitators. This setup provides the learners with innumerable samples of authentic communication as the facilitators will naturally interact with each

---

5   The term 'facilitator' will be used throughout this volume instead of *teacher* as a constant reminder of the quintessentially supportive and non-authoritarian role of the SLE course designer and initiator.

6   The concept of authentication, borrowed from Leo Van Lier (1996) is discussed at a number of points later in this volume.

other as well as with the learners – always in the target language. Hence, students will be exposed to a great deal of natural linguistic – and extra-linguistic – interaction (phonetic, syntactic, morphological, lexical, pragmatic, proxemic and gestural), much like that available to virtually every child as it bootstraps itself into its native tongue.

Conventional classroom instruction, drills and de-situated exercises play no significant role in these initiatory emergence settings [just as such highly contrived didactic practices are virtually absent from environments in which children start to develop communicative competence in their native tongue(s)]. But learners in SLE courses are invited and encouraged to work with (and even seek out for themselves) instructional materials outside of class (online for example), should they feel the need for explicit deductive rules to supplement the highly communicative activities that take place in class. The idea is that grammar and lexis are learned first and foremost through communicative interaction itself during highly authentic, interactive and monolingual class sessions, but that grammar can and should also be efficiently and effectively reinforced through consciousness-raising sessions and self-study, particularly in the case of adult learners.

In addition to focusing on the specifically linguistic aspects of communication, SLE principles emphasise the value of viewing language as an *embodied* phenomenon. James Asher's *Total Physical Response* technique (a key pedagogical tool that was incorporated into Krashen's *Natural Approach*) is used extensively in the SLE courses we run at the FTSK, particularly in the early stages, to reacquaint learners with the embodied-learning competence they developed extensively as children in learning their native language[7].

Courses based on this *Scaffolded Language Emergence* approach have been created and run at the FTSK to provide students with an emergent introduction to no fewer than 13 languages (Mandarin, French, Spanish, Portuguese, Hungarian, Russian, Gaelic, Modern Greek, German, Italian, Dutch, Arabic and Farsi). With few exceptions[8], I have provided extensive guidance to all of

---

7   Embodiment is addressed in Chapter 3 in the discussion of SGAV methodology.
8   The one notable exception is Dutch. Two lecturers in Dutch at the FTSK (Caroline Jacobs-Henkel and Rianne Fuchs-Franke) adopted the SLE approach after a workshop I offered in 2008 for faculty at the School interested in the 'B1 in nine-months' project. But they developed a method for Dutch that is fully in line with the approach as outlined in this volume – without subsequent coaching from me. The method they developed has been used for the past eight years to bring all new students of Dutch who enrol in the BA program for translators at the FTSK to at least the B1 or B2 level within one semester.

the teachers in understanding the principles of the approach and have accompanied their initial course-design efforts, despite having no prior knowledge of most of these languages myself. I have also attended numerous class sessions of all of the courses offered (except for those offered in the Dutch programme) and have offered extensive feedback and advice to help the facilitators develop expertise in using the approach.

It should be clear at this point that the SLE approach has been developed specifically as an approach for initiating and scaffolding only at the very earliest stages of second language emergence, that is for guiding and accompanying students up to and through the threshold at which the newly emergent language becomes an incipiently self-generating and self-maintaining (autopoietic) system. At that point, we have found that learning and acquisition can proceed on the basis of any number of approaches, perhaps even ones largely dependent on conventional instruction. As mentioned earlier in this chapter, however, a similarly humanistic and post-method approach like Dogme would appear to be the ideal way to follow up on an introductory SLE course. The new language can be expected to continue to emerge once the learner has adopted a proactive approach to 'bootstrapping' and fomenting his or her own appropriation of the new second language in a monolingual (target language) environment.

Chapter 2: Initial steps towards the SLE approach

> *As a child, you talked with your significant others about things of shared interest using words and phrases that came to mind, and all the while you learned language.* (Ellis et al. 2015, p. 63)

'TELC B1 in nine months': The project that set the stage for the SLE approach

This book is not about translation studies or translator education. Instead, it is about an approach to initiating, promoting and enhancing second language emergence that happens to have been developed, applied and tested at a school of translation studies at a university. Students who begin their studies in the field of translation and interpretation often, if not usually, have been exposed to instruction in one or more of the small set of languages that can be offered in secondary school programs. The language emergence approach presented here was originally designed to offer an initiation into languages that students have not had an opportunity to learn prior to enrolling at university. A key premise upon which this book is based is that the approach outlined here should be similarly well suited to adults who are not studying to become translators. While the idea of immersion in language teaching is hardly new, it has almost always been applied to classes for young children, for example in the St. Lambert approach that was developed and first implemented in Quebec in the 1960s.

A primary assumption of that particular approach was that the ability to acquire a foreign language naturally diminished rapidly with increasing age (Wesche 2002). The SLE approach, on the other hand, assumes that a foreign language can also emerge in adults, and with great success in terms of achieving a high level of communicative competence. While Steven Krashen's *Natural Approach* (1982) was also created ostensibly to promote foreign language learning in adults, it will be shown throughout this volume that these two approaches are based on radically different epistemological principles and theoretical assumptions and are hence incommensurable. In developing SLE, I did draw on my own experience using the *Natural Approach* to teach Spanish at the University of Illinois in 1986, but, as I hope will be made clear throughout this book, my understanding of the nature of language learning has evolved considerably since that time. This means that I do not see SLE as an attempt to revive the *Natural Approach*; instead, I believe it proposes a radically different perspective on the nature of naturalistic elementary language learning.

Translation Studies at the FTSK of the University of Mainz, Germany, has a long and noteworthy history dating back to 1947. For decades, it has been one of the largest translator education programmes in the world and it currently offers degrees in translation and/or interpretation in as many as 13 languages. But while research at the FTSK, for example in the areas of translation theory, cognitive translation processes, translation-related corpus linguistics, and translation and interpreting didactics has been voluminous and influential, second language instruction at the institution was restricted largely to versions of the *Grammar-Translation method* until just after the turn of the millennium. It was then that the School's semi-official language centre was established with the objective of offering more communicative extra-curricular language instruction at the FTSK parallel to the regular translation studies curriculum. In 2008, the 'B1 in nine months' project was initiated[9] to develop a teaching approach that would be better suited than the *Grammar-Translation method* to the development of communicative competence for language mediators-in-training.

Having completed an MA and a PhD in language teaching and teacher education, I had the good fortune to be one of just two language teaching specialists on the FTSK faculty at that time (along with Dr. Ursula Hassel), and soon found myself with the task of 1) designing a teaching approach that would enable students starting from zero in a second, third or fourth language to achieve at least a B1 level of competence in that language within nine months, and 2) training graduate students to create and run these language courses in their respective native languages.

The B1 project grew out of the realisation that the existing – almost exclusively content-, textbook-, syllabus- and teacher-centred – methods used to teach the panoply of languages offered at the School were no longer in tune with the prevailing view of translation as a largely communicative activity

---

9 This programme designed to revamp elementary language teaching praxis at the FTSK was initiated and managed by Dr. Ursula Hassel under the direction of Prof. Andreas Kelletat.

rather than one essentially involving linguistic recoding. And yet, even within the domain of language teaching per se, positivist epistemologies and structure-focused teaching have retained a strong grip on teaching, despite tremendous efforts and great progress in research on language teaching methodology.

It is important to note that, while the SLE approach outlined here initially evolved largely on the basis of a few language teaching methodologies I had encountered essentially by chance and my personal experience using and studying them, an entire sub-field of language acquisition studies has emerged that has started to provide extensive empirical and theoretical support to the approach – without having been used to create it. 'Usage-based' language development studies have been investigating various aspects of language structure and also acquisition from an 'emergentist' (autopoietic) perspective that overlaps significantly with my understanding of language as an emergent phenomenon. To summarise this position in a nutshell, as Tomasello has written:

> The usage-based theory of language acquisition makes the fundamental claim that language structure emerges from language use. This applies at the level of individual words, as their communicative function derives from their use, as well as at the level of grammar, as structure emerges from patterns of use of multi-unit utterances. (Tomasello 2011: 254)

The belief that non-native languages must be taught on the basis of imparted rules persists — and this in the face of overwhelming evidence to the contrary from studies on first language development. We are all surely aware that children throughout the world acquire the ability to use their mother tongue for extensive communicative purposes within the first few years of their lives without formal instruction and without resorting to descriptive or prescriptive language rules. Within those first few years, significant mastery of the mother tongue is achieved by virtually all L1 learners in all cultures through experiential interaction with the environment, mediated via communicative interaction with other speakers of the language at hand. The rules of the mother tongue are not memorised, drilled, or tested; they appear to be constructed by each individual in unique, personal, experiential communion in context and with other members of society.

While the assumption that communicative competence emerges from usage set the initial epistemological stage for the creation of the B1 project courses at the FTSK, I was still faced with the task of creating an overall approach that could be readily adapted to the many languages that were to be taught, for which there were no off-the-shelf teaching materials, and for courses that would be designed and run almost exclusively by inexperienced language teachers who would have little time to be trained in how to create or run language courses.

The teaching staff were to be almost exclusively students of translation enrolled at the School and native speakers of the languages they would be teaching. Only a few departments took full advantage of the project and in the end, 'B1 in nine months' courses were offered only in Spanish, Russian, Hungarian and Dutch. Shorter intensive courses with more modest communicative competence targets were run as part of the project in Modern Greek, Korean, Farsi, Arabic, Chinese, Portuguese, Italian, English and German.

In preparing the pedagogical framework for our project, I chose to develop my own approach, on the basis of which courses would be designed [10] by teams of facilitators for the various introductory language courses that were to be developed and implemented within the scope of the B1 project – and presumably beyond. The disadvantage in terms of the amount of time and effort needed for each team to create a syllabus and teaching techniques as well as to gather authentic teaching materials would presumably be considerable. On the other hand, it meant that each team of facilitators would benefit from the opportunity to actually design a course themselves, including the materials to be used and the pedagogical techniques to be applied in running the classes. Rather than serving as mere teaching technicians, their role would be much more like educational designer-implementers, tasked with using a coherent set of principles to design the courses they would then facilitate. This was expected to be (and would in fact prove to be) a very useful exercise in competence- and confidence building on the part of the student facilitators.

My early experiences with language learning and sources of inspiration for SLE

Having now set the stage for the development of a pedagogical approach that would be suited to the 'B1 in nine months' project, in Chapter 3 I will turn the clock back a few decades to the 1970s and '80s and outline some of my experiences with the two teaching approaches that have had the greatest influence on the development of the SLE approach. My personal views of language teaching

---

10 Based on Richards & Rodgers distinction between 'approach' and 'method'.

and learning have naturally been greatly influenced by my own experience with language teaching approaches and methods, both as a learner and teacher.

I personally got off to a less than auspicious start as a language learner in school. My experience learning foreign languages began in 1961 when I participated in the innovative FLES program for early language learning that was being implemented at the time in public schools in the greater Cleveland, Ohio area (Diekhoff 1965). I remember that first year of French (when I was in second grade), which was taught using the – at that time new and innovative – audio-lingual method, as being quite enjoyable, but the novelty of learning a new language wore off quickly. Years later, having failed to acquire more than a modicum of communicative capability in French (or even the slightest intrinsic motivation for learning the language) in six years of instruction in elementary and secondary school, I found myself in a Spanish-for-beginners class in my second year of high school in 1970. It was with a distinct sense of déjà vu that I realised two years later at the end of high school that the instruction I had received in Spanish had left me with no communicative competence in the language whatsoever.

But then, while pursuing a BA in political science in the mid-1970s, I was forced by the undergraduate language requirement to again try my hand at French during my third and fourth years at university. For reasons that I still do not fathom, particularly given the ineffectual, purely instructional, teaching approach that was used once again at the university level, I surprised myself by feeling more motivated to learn more of the language – and better – this time around. Then, having discovered an interest in the language and culture during those two years, I continued to take French courses the following year while pursuing a master's degree in International Affairs at Florida State University. My unexpected success at learning French in those three years of classes at university, and an exchange agreement between Florida State and an engineering college in France, paved the way for me to move to France, where I not only became fluent in French within a matter of months, but where I would be employed at an engineering college as an English instructor without any prior training or experience in language teaching. This sink-or-swim experience would prove to be a watershed experience that convinced me that foreign languages can indeed be learned in the classroom. It all depends on how would-be teachers and learners go about it.

Chapter 3: *Structuro-Global Audio-Visual (SGAV)* methodology: a partially successful attempt to shift from an instructionist to a constructivist epistemology

It was in 1977, as a result of my newfound personal interest in French language and culture, that I found myself in Lyons, France, teaching English as a *lecteur d'anglais* at the *Institut National des Sciences Appliquées* (INSA). Up to that point, I had had no training whatsoever as a language teacher. *Lecteurs* were hired by INSA at that time to give engineering students the opportunity to hone their English language skills in classes run by native English speakers. No instruction or training at all was provided for new teachers; the existing staff gave us a few tips on what to do in our classes (which involved either working through exercises in a textbook at lower levels or leading guided conversation sessions for more advanced students), and that was it. Along with my regular teaching load at INSA, I also found a part-time evening job teaching English to adults at a private language school nearby. There, I was given a copy of the student's book, a set of filmstrips and audio tapes and was sent into the classroom to teach English. The method was entitled: *English by the Audio Visual Method* (Filipovic et. al. 1962) and seemed to bear an uncanny resemblance to the audio-visual method that had been imposed on me in my second-grade elementary French class in Cleveland, Ohio – in 1962!

As luck would have it, I was introduced to this first generation *Structuro-Global Audio-Visual* method right about the time that second-generation *SGAV* methods were coming on the market, so I found myself introduced to a first generation *SGAV* method (based on a methodology that had begun to be developed in the 1950s) in the fall of 1977. To put it bluntly: the method was clearly showing its age at that time. But it was only a few months later that I had the good luck of being introduced to the *All's Well* method (levels I & II), an encounter that would leave an indelible mark on me and my teaching praxis.

It was in fact at that same private language school where *All's Well* came in to replace the first generation method within a few months of my arrival in Lyons. When a one-week introductory training seminar was offered by the school in the fall of 1977, I signed up. What took place in that first of several week-long seminars I attended has helped guide my thinking on second language learning and my educational practice and research ever since. In fact, aspects of many of the learning activities incorporated into that seminar have found their way in one form or another into the SLE approach I have created at the FTSK in Germersheim – as well as into my collaborative approach to translator education (Kiraly 2000).

When we arrived for the first workshop session, the approximately 20 participants, some French, some American and some British teachers of English (a few with pedagogical training, most not), found ourselves in a carpeted room with no chairs, tables, pictures or anything at all but a reel-to-reel tape recorder and a filmstrip projector. There was also a gentleman named Richard who introduced himself as the *animateur* (a designation that I came to understand as referring to a role far more akin to that of a facilitator of learning than a conventional teacher). He introduced himself briefly and then, without further ado, asked us to stand around the sides of the room. We were then asked to choose a spot somewhere at eye level on the opposite wall and then, accompanied by soothing background music, we spent the next five minutes or so walking back and forth across the room. We first walked slowly, eyes focused only on the spot ahead of us. We then chose another spot and walked back. We also tried walking backwards across the room, then with our eyes shut, then moving our outstretched arms in circles as we walked.

This was the first of several hours of activities that day during which we spoke very little, but moved and interacted a great deal. During a group discussion at the end of the morning (one that was reiterated several times over the course of the week-long workshop) about what we were experiencing and learning, we came to realise that what may have originally seemed like childish games were in fact initial steps toward re-acculturation, towards becoming members of the *All's Well* community of teachers and, at the same time, steps toward seeing language learning as an activity that could benefit from activities extending far beyond conventional exercises. These steps proved to be essential for our understanding of how language learning or acquisition can be fostered in a classroom setting – essentially by reinserting the physical and emotional factors involved in natural learning that tend to be ignored by conventional, teacher- and textbook-centred teaching approaches.

Over the course of that week, in addition to working with the *All's Well* audio-visual course materials, we experienced numerous interactive and ludic activities for focusing on relaxation, concentration and perception, movement, mime, gestures, and space utilisation – as well as language development. While at the beginning, most of the seminar participants were occasionally puzzled and perhaps even a bit embarrassed by some of those non-academic activities, within a few days the underlying structure of the method was becoming self-evident, and a sense of community and trust as well as an appreciation for this uniquely humanistic approach to learning and teaching soon pervaded the atmosphere in our classroom.

Starting out as separate individuals seeking to learn how to use the *All's Well* teaching method, we gradually merged, with the assistance of Richard, into a community of incipient *All's Well* teachers through a multi-faceted series of interpersonal activities. In hindsight, it was clear that our seminar leader did not attempt to instruct us per se; instead he set the stage for activities which allowed us to develop the skills necessary to use the *All's Well* English development method and he guided group discussions in which the participants' voices were at the centre of attention rather than his. We did not have the impression of being trained as such – instead we found ourselves in one collaborative and communicative situation after another. We could experience the approach for ourselves and we could use our natural physical, emotional and social faculties to interact with other members of our emerging community, we could relax when we were under stress, concentrate when we were distracted and communicate non-verbally when we were at a loss for words. In the end, it would be those hours spent exploring a new approach to understanding language learning and facilitating, a new pedagogical language and culture, that would leave that indelible mark on me – rather than the *All's Well* method itself.

The *All's Well* teaching materials, which we also explored collaboratively over the course of the week, consisted – just as the *English with the Audio-Visual Method* did – of a sequence of audio-visual filmstrips and accompanying audio tapes. But the scenarios that the filmstrips and accompanying audio tapes depicted in this new method were amusing, colourful and lively. In both cases, they were used to provide initial input for learners' personal construction processes. The cartoon characters in the *All's Well* dialogues spoke at an almost normal conversational speed and exhibited a myriad of gestures, postures, moods and attitudes. And the stories followed a progression of interpersonal as well as linguistic complexity. The initial presentation of the filmstrips was global in nature – with no dissection of the language involved. Subsequent analytical activities focused on sharpening awareness of supra-segmental features of English as well as identifying morphological, lexical and syntactic structures of the language. Linguistic jargon and language rules, however, were completely banished from classroom activities.

Work on prosodic features of English included, for example: walking while characters spoke and stopping when they paused; tapping a tambourine to the rhythm of a text read aloud, and attempting to follow an intonation curve with the whole body. Learners (and we also, as prospective *All's Well* teachers) were dissuaded from using French in class because it was felt that this would interfere with the somato-cognitive development of the new language. The students, however, were never to be forced to speak English upon command. It was understood that learners need different amounts of time to process the new language and that they would speak when they were ready to do so.

Principles of SGAV methodology

Here I would like to include the perspective of the creators of *All's Well* to help present the principles underlying it. In this section, I have included some short passages quoted directly from the *All's Well That Starts Well* teacher's manual (Dickinson et. al, 1975), followed respectively by my own comments that elucidate how I interpreted the principles for my own classroom facilitating practice[11]. I found each and every one of these principles reflected in the *All's Well* teacher-training workshops I attended in Lyons in 1978, even though, as I will discuss toward the end of this chapter, it was not always easy to apply the principles as I had understood them to the lessons proposed in the teaching materials:

> Communication of course is much wider than words and expressions; it includes the body, the time and space that surrounds each of us. A second language is a living, moving entity … From the very start the second language must envelope the student … Language is not the manipulation of tongue, teeth, hard and soft palates … Language is the whole body. When we express ourselves we use affective melodies, intonations, pauses, rhythms, gestures, facial expressions and physical movements. It is "I" who am speaking, both body and spirit. (Dickinson et. al. 1976: 16)

---

11 These passages from Dickinson et. al, 1975) were quoted before in Kiraly, 2000: p. 175-176. They have been requoted here because they are particularly germane in this context.

To me, this meant that instead of having learners sitting passively behind desks listening to the teacher talk at them, it is essential for course facilitators to encourage learners to use all of their senses as they begin to learn how to communicate through the new Ln[12]. Activities that motivate students to explore the use of the senses and bodily activity in communication (for example by moving in response to language or to accompany language, using gestures to specify or complement linguistic meaning, drawing pictures, and participating in games and role-play) can encourage them to use for communicative benefit all of the dimensions of perception, action and learning with which they are naturally endowed.

The *All's Well* authors emphasise this point later on in the handbook:

In their own native language, the students will automatically use the right melodies and gestures to accompany their enunciations. When it comes to learning a second language, however, we find that there is a conviction that physical involvement is not necessary and, secondly, a certain embarrassment when expressing oneself in front of others. A precondition to effective language learning seems to be that adults must again learn the use of their body in the second language. (ibid: 20)

Therefore, adult learners may well need assistance to revive their naturally interwoven multi-faceted learning skills (cognitive, emotional and corporeal) as they begin to explore the Ln that is beginning to emerge within them. While some will surely resist due to years of experience as passive learners in scholastic settings, helping them re-appropriate their dormant somatic faculties will be invaluable for fostering the emergence of the Ln.

Learners also need to be bathed in the sounds, gestures and proxemic features of the new language. The learners' prior knowledge of one or more languages (in all its facets) naturally means that SGAV course participants had already learned a great deal about how languages can be structured and how they can function, and they are already familiar with innumerable skills for making sense of the world and communicating with others. Nonetheless, overt use of languages other than the emergent one can be a significant distraction and a hindrance to Ln language emergence. Hence, the learners' native tongue was understood to have no place in the SGAV classroom. By leaving it outside

---

12 Based on analogy with L1 and L2, Ln will be used throughout this volume to refer to any language that may be emerging within a learner at a given time.

the class, so to speak, even adult students can be expected to have a far easier time becoming acculturated into a new language community.

> To ask a student to produce exactly the same quality and quantity in their language expression as they have received in their language comprehension is tantamount to asking them to speak in words that are not yet their own. … comprehension is the basis upon which students will be able to build their expression. (ibid: 18)

The authors of *All's Well* claim that our capability for comprehending a language is always greater than our ability to express ourselves in it, which intuitively seems to be a plausible assumption. This assumption, expressed as C>e (comprehension is greater than expression), must be respected in the Ln classroom. Not only must care be taken to avoid expecting students to spit back features of their Ln immediately after being exposed to them in class, learners must be given time to structure the language for themselves and at their own pace. The 'teach x – memorise x – regurgitate x' didactic sequence so familiar from conventional learning approaches must give way to providing samples of comprehensible language that naturally pave the way for personal language construction. Each learner starts to produce language when he or she is ready – and not necessarily right when the teacher demands it.

> [...] teaching has the task of bathing the student in a variety of language sounds and linguistic data, but it is the student who has to organize them, it is the students alone who can structure the language for themselves … There are innumerable different ways to organize and structure; we could even say that each individual has his or her own unique, personal way to do it. (ibid: 28)

Language will emerge differently in each individual and each group of learners. Each individual of course represents a wealth of unique personal experiences and history, personality features, cognitive capabilities and interests. This must be taken into account in the creation of Ln courses.

Beyond intracranial cognition: the thread of embodiment running through *SGAV* methodology

Learning about *All's Well* and *SGAV* methodology taught me that rather than being a purely intra-cranial cognitive process, language use and communicative competence are *embodied*, that is, intimately connected to our multi-facetted emotional and physical as well as cognitive selves. We know intuitively that our mood, motivation, gestures, tone of voice, intonation and rhythm and even our use of personal space can carry meaning. As Douglas Robinson (1991) points out, we often react intuitively, even viscerally to language in use:

> Our bodies often react to language use that seems different, deviant, somehow 'wrong', with anxiety signals: there is a twinge in the chest, or a slight constriction of the throat. Most people do not know the rules that would allow them to define the triggering usage as "wrong" in any systematic, grammatical sense. But it feels wrong. It clashes with the body conditioning that they have for that usage or that context, with the ideosomatics of syntax, semantics, stylistics. "Bad grammar" feels wrong. (p. 13)

This viewpoint is supported by the 'somatic marker' hypothesis formulated by the neuroscientist Antonio Damasio to help explain the interplay of emotions and logic in reasoning (Damasio 1994: 174):

> Somatic markers are special instance feelings generated from secondary emotions. Those emotions and feelings have been connected, by learning, to predicted future outcomes of certain scenarios. When a negative somatic marker is juxtaposed to a particular future outcome, the combination functions as an alarm bell. When a positive somatic marker is juxtaposed instead, it becomes a beacon of incentive.

Damasio's book *Descartes' Error* set out to refute René Descartes' concept of mind/body duality, and to demonstrate the key integrated role that emotions and the body play in ordinary cognitive processes. In the Cartesian tradition, the cognitivist epistemology that is still prevalent in educational institutions, attempts to neatly separate the mind from the body and the emotions, focusing almost exclusively on the first while virtually ignoring the latter.

In this context, Robinson (1991: 16) notes that:

Part of learning a language well is watching what native speakers' bodies do when they speak it: how they move their mouths, how they gesture and shift their weight, how they stumble over words, where and how they pause, how they use stress for emphasis – in general, how they stage their speech. But even that will not be enough if it is done mechanically, if you simply observe native speakers' bodies and mimic them. You have to do more than watch; you have to intuit, sense what their bodies are doing inside, sense how they feel when they speak.

Within a genuine social setting, the individual can be viewed as constructing a personal version (idiolect) of the language of the community through collaborative interaction with peers and more knowledgeable others. Learning in an authentic communicative setting through genuine, embodied interaction, is inherently a personal holistic experience for each learner; it is intricately interwoven with that learner's needs, desires, emotions and stages of psychological as well as linguistic development. Varela, Thompson and Roche (1991) went a step further in suggesting that cognition is not only embodied but *enacted*. This represents a major step towards ecological thinking, which has been applied to foreign language education perhaps most extensively by Van Lier (1996). The essential idea is that the individual mind is not merely situated in a pre-determined setting, subject to the imperatives imposed on it by a pre-existent world. Instead, from this viewpoint, cognition is seen as being dependent on the synergistic interaction between the mind and the environment, not in depicting or reflecting the world as it is, but in the world making. (See also Goodman 1978)

These assumptions, all explicitly integrated into second generation *SGAV* methodology, have also been incorporated into the SLE approach to Ln development.

SGAV: Conflict between the philosophy and the methodology

One might ask at this point why, if I was so taken with *All's Well* principles right from the start of my language teaching career, it would not have made sense to simply adopt this methodology for use within the scope of the 'B1 in nine months' project at the University of Mainz. As it turned out, in 1980, when I returned to the US to pursue a degree in the teaching of French at the University of Illinois, *SGAV* was at the apex of its popularity in Europe, but within just a few years, interest in using *All's Well* was very much on the decline and it faded into virtual oblivion in the 1980s. The problem, as I see it, was considerable conflict on the epistemological level. The developers of *SGAV* claim to have drawn heavily on Gestalt psychology[13] in establishing the epistemological base of the approach. The holistic qualities of this psychological approach indeed seemed in line with the philosophy behind the teachers' training courses that I attended in 1978 as well as the consensus views on learning and teaching that emerged in the community of *All's Well* practitioners with whom I worked in Lyons. And yet, the method itself and the lesson plans imposed on teachers were extremely rigid. The lessons all adopted the same procedures in a precise order (Rivenc 2003):

1. Global presentation of a new lesson based on a film-strip or other audio-visual material
2. Dissection of the lesson into smaller units and discussion of those elements to ensure adequate comprehension
3. Choral repetition of elements presented in the lesson
4. Pseudo-communicative activities in which the learned elements were to be applied in similar (and similarly contrived) contexts

The vocabulary presented in the lessons was carefully preselected on the basis of surveys of the most frequent words required for basic communication in the language being introduced. The topics to be introduced in class were to be strictly limited to those presented in the textbook and in fact, neither the teachers nor the learners had much say in the language that would be used or ostensibly learned in class. Ivan (2006) attributes these features of the *SGAV* approach and methods to the underlying behaviourist foundation of the approach. In fact, the first generation of *SGAV* methods was developed already in the 1950s during the heyday of the audio-lingual method in the US, and at a time when behaviourism was the dominant psychological paradigm. Having taught using both first and second generation *SGAV* methods, it was apparent to me that an attempt was made between the two generations to effectuate a major pedagogical shift in the approach. But the lesson plans imposed on *All's*

---

13 Gestalt psychology is a philosophy of mind that originated at the Berlin School of experimental psychology. Gestalt psychology purports seek an understanding of the laws behind the ability to acquire and maintain meaningful perceptions in what appears to be a chaotic world. The essential principle of gestalt psychology is that the mind forms a global whole with self-organizing tendencies. [See Smith (1988)].

Well teachers and learners seemed to reflect a certain reluctance to make a commitment to the bold step forward suggested by the tenor and contents of the training workshops. The incipient new paradigm, focused on learner-centred instruction, learner autonomy, and authentic communication was the hallmark of the 'communicative' approaches that were coming to the fore at that time on both sides of the Atlantic. At this point, my experiment with *SGAV* began to wind down and fate took me back to the US and new language teaching experiences.

In the next chapter, we will take a look at Steven Krashen's *Natural Approach*, which incorporates James Asher's *Total Physical Response* technique precisely as a way to ensure that a language acquired in the classroom will serve as that essential naturalistic link between the language being acquired by the learner and the physical world in which the learner is embedded and embodied. This was the second major methodological approach to foreign language teaching that I worked with extensively and that had a major impact on the development of SLE.

Chapter 4: The *Natural Approach:* comprehensible input and a cognitivist epistemology

Over the course of the year following my initial *All's Well* seminar, I attended several advanced workshops on the method and also had the opportunity to apply it in team-teaching fashion in many classes for adult students, primarily in university-run continuing education classes for engineers and private-school group classes for business executives. In 1980, I left France and *All's Well* behind (even though I did have further opportunities to use the method again when I returned to Europe in 1981 and spent two years teaching English with *All's Well* and other methods in Lyons and Roanne, France and in Gijón, Spain).

Upon returning to the US in 1980 to pursue graduate study in second language education at the University of Illinois, I found the essence of the *All's Well* principles that had become my pedagogical beacons (they were called "guiding lights" in the *All's Well* teachers' manual) echoed in the *Communicative Language Teaching* revolution that was well under way at the time on the other side of the Atlantic. Communicative language teaching in the US essentially began with Sandra Savignon's now classic dissertation (1971). As fate would have it, I found myself working as a research assistant to Professor Savignon during my MA programme, and she became my primary dissertation advisor when I returned to the University of Illinois to undertake my doctoral studies in 1986. By that time, the *Natural Approach*, created by Stephen Krashen and Tracy Terrell, had taken elementary language teaching at the university level in the US by storm and in 1996, Erwin Tschirner, a co-author of *Kontakte*, the *Natural Approach* textbook for German, wrote that "the Natural Approach [...] has become one of the most widely used communicative methodologies in second language departments across North America" (1996: 50).

The *Natural Approach* had been developed in the mid-1970s specifically as an approach for use in introductory second language classes at American universities. The goal of the approach was to develop primarily communicative rather than grammatical competence (that is, the ability to use language for genuine communicative purposes rather than being merely familiar with linguistic descriptions of features of the language). After publishing an initial article outlining the approach, Tracy Terrell began working with Steven Krashen, who had just come out with his 'Monitor Model' of second language acquisition, a theory that emphasises the difference between, on the one hand, learning (defined as deductive, conscious and rule-based) and acquisition (which Krashen hypothesised was intuitive and experiential). Krashen saw the 'monitor' as a function of the LAD (Language Acquisition Device) that comprised (deductive and overt) learning. While he saw (intuitively) acquired language as the fountain of utterances, he claimed that the monitor supervised language production and intervened after the fact to correct utterances deemed faulty by the LAD on the basis of learned knowledge about the language.

The *Natural Approach* appears to draw on the Piagetian concept of stages of development as well as Chomskyan cognitivism, but its overt theoretical foundation is the set of five hypotheses proposed by Krashen (which, as mentioned in Chapter 1, have drawn a great deal of criticism from scholars in the field of second language acquisition studies because of the lack of evidence found to support them and their allegedly unfalsifiable nature):

1. *Acquisition versus learning hypothesis*: There are two different ways to develop communicative competence in a language: 1) acquisition – a subconscious, natural process, identical to the one children use when learning their mother tongue before they go to school; and 2) learning – a conscious process that entails the ingestion and understanding of rules of how the language functions.
2. *Natural Order hypothesis:* Second language rules are acquired in a fixed order, determined by innate mechanisms and not by linguistic complexity or explicit teaching.
3. *Monitor Hypothesis:* The monitor involves a supervisory system of learned knowledge about a language that watches over spontaneous language production (which Krashen claims is produced from acquired knowledge). The monitor interferes to correct (on the basis of learned rules) language mistakes made by the acquisitional system during communicative events.
4. *Input Hypothesis:* This explains the essence of the acquisitional process. A second language is acquired (according to Krashen) by processing comprehensible input, that is, input that has been attended to and understood. For acquisition to take place, the input has to be slightly superior to the level of the learner (i+1) and comprehensible. Acquisition is carried out by an innate mechanism (the Language Acquisition Device – LAD).

5. *Affective Filter Hypothesis*: This is something of a misnomer as it is not seen as 'filtering' anything. Instead, it is more like a barrier that rises when the learner has negative feelings of stress, incompetence or lack of motivation. In Krashen's view, teachers can lower this filter (or barrier) by enhancing learners' feelings of comfort and self-esteem in the classroom, thereby reducing a major hindrance to acquisition.

While Krashen and Terrell were in some disagreement about certain aspects of learning and acquisition, for example the precise nature of the distinction between conscious and sub-conscious learning and the value of teaching grammar rules, they nevertheless shared a common core of principles that can be seen to be compatible with the *All's Well* principles outlined in Chapter 3. The NA principles were summarised as follows by Tschirner (1996):

1. The second language is taught and learned as discourse, with a focus on authentic interaction rather than on the exemplification of language usage. The students' native tongue is seen as disruptive and is all but excluded from classroom interaction.
2. The content of classroom interaction focuses on the needs and interests of the students and the foreign-language environment.
3. The primary forms of classroom interaction are pair and small-group work.
4. Perception precedes production; both are seen and treated as independent skills.
5. Care is taken both in perception and in production to ensure that words and phrases are properly stored.
6. Affective factors receive particular attention.
7. The use of media plays a major role, both for affective and socio-cultural reasons, and in order to place special emphasis on listening comprehension.

In the *Natural Approach* (as in the *SGAV* methods, including *All's Well*), instruction involves the almost exclusive use of interaction in which the focus of attention is on communication, rather than on linguistic form. In both approaches, grammatical competence is expected to largely take care of itself if learners are motivated to interact communicatively. The originators of both approaches specify that interaction in the classroom should revolve around topics that are of personal interest to the students as well as aspects of the foreign culture.

The teacher and the students in a *Natural Approach* classroom are expected to speak only the second language during classroom activities. The teacher's primary tasks are to 1) provide comprehensible input, which Krashen saw as the grist for the learner's language acquisition mill (LAD), and 2) put students in situations in which they can work cooperatively to discover and acquire the ability to use the second language competently. The emphasis is on the acquisition of basic communicative skills, with comprehension preceding expression, and oral/aural skills preceding use of the written language.

The role of affective factors was as important in the *Natural Approach* as it was in the *All's Well* method. In the *Natural Approach*, Krashen's concept of the 'affective filter' comes into play. He hypothesised that the more stressful the learning situation, the less able learners are to acquire the features of the second language. Some decades after the *Natural Approach* was introduced and without referring specifically to Krashen's affective filter, Ferro summarised the role of affective factors in learning as follows:

> [...] the body produces one type of hormone when a stressful situation is seen as a challenge (distress) and a different type of hormone when the stressful situation is seen as a threat (distress) to a person's capability to function and the stressor appears inescapable. Thus the emotional response of the individual to a specific situation plays a determining role in that person's cognitive functioning – either to fight, resist, or avoid the learning situation or to be open to new opportunities. (1993: p. 32)

Consequently, the *Natural Approach* teacher tries to create an environment that promotes intuitive *acquisition*, encouraging the development of a community in the classroom and avoiding overt correction, while promoting meaningful and enjoyable interaction among the learners. The physical dimension of language acquisition is addressed through the use of *Total Physical Response* (TPR), a technique developed by James Asher (1977). TPR essentially involves having learners follow commands to carry out actions in the classroom in the early stages of second language learning in order to activate motor memory and to somatically grasp the potential meanings of second language structures, much as infants do as they begin to acquire their mother tongue.

The Whole Language Movement

At first glance, the assumptions upon which second generation *SGAV* methodology appears to be based (at least when we look at the documentation for teachers prepared by the authors of *All's Well* and the perspective communicated during the teacher training sessions that I attended in Lyons) seem to be very much in line with those underlying the *Natural Approach* as well. And in turn, both sets of assumptions appear to be very much in line with the principles underlying the *Whole Language Movement*, which emerged in the 1980s as a general pedagogical approach guiding, in particular, language arts in elementary and secondary schools in Australia and New Zealand. In a nutshell:

> The consensus on the fundamental features of the philosophy includes (1) that language develops naturally and is therefore a social phenomenon used for communication purposes, (2) that language learning and teaching must be personalized in order to meet the needs and interest of each learner, and (3) that language learning is considered to be a part of making sense of the world; language therefore does not need to be learned separately first, but rather is learned holistically in context, not in bits and pieces in isolation (Froese 1991: 2).

The principles underlying 'whole language' are paraphrased below:
- Language, both written and oral, is most easily learned within contexts of use. Learners acquire the ability to control linguistic processes if they encounter holistic, relevant and functional language in the accomplishment of real purposes.
- A major task of the language teacher is to involve learners in relevant functional activities and experiences that will stretch their capabilities. Teachers should mediate learners' transactions with the world and support learning, but without controlling it. They should help learners find opportunities that encourage them to collaboratively address a variety of problems that are important and meaningful to them.
- Authentic activities in which language serves in real and functional ways are always stressed.
- Rather than being learned by imitating teachers or learning decontextualised rules, language is invented by each individual, and it is adapted to social conventions in the context of actual language use.

- Whole-language teachers are leaders in the classroom; they do not abdicate their authority or responsibility. They lead by virtue of their greater experience, their knowledge, and their respect for their pupils. They know their pupils, monitor their learning, and provide support and resources as they are needed. They understand that there must be collaboration and a relationship of trust between themselves and their pupils if an effective learning atmosphere is to be created.

In essence, these are principles common to what we might call humanistic approaches to language teaching, with the acknowledgement that language is constructed in a more inductive way rather than being derived deductively from rules, and with an emphasis on learner empowerment, learner motivation for learning, and learners' needs. As noted at the conclusion to the chapter on *SGAV* methodology, however, the actual praxis of applying an approach in the classroom can be very much at odds with the philosophy.

My shift from being a committed *All's Well* teacher to being a committed *Natural Approach* teacher was virtually seamless. At the time (1986), I was far more concerned with what I was doing in the classroom in terms of helping students learn than with the epistemological underpinnings of the respective approach I was using. In fact, I do not think my teaching approach changed much at all when I went from *SGAV* teaching at INSA in Lyons to using the *Natural Approach* at the University of Illinois. Over the intervening 30 years, however, as I have moved away from seeing the primary role of the language teacher as that of an efficient user of a teaching method to that of a designer of a pedagogical encounter that can foment and support language emergence, I have come to have a great appreciation for pedagogical epistemology – philosophical perspectives on what it means to know and to learn. It is on this level, I believe, that we can find important distinctions between methods and approaches, distinctions that may have a profound impact on how we see the roles of teachers and learners, and of teaching and learning in language classrooms.

Epistemological incommensurability: Vygotskyan Social Constructivism and the *Natural Approach*

In *A Social Constructivist Approach to Translator Education* (Kiraly 2000), I identified the social constructivism of Lev Vygotsky as a plausible epistemology for the development of a collaborative project-based approach to translator education. The longest chapter in the book deals with foreign language learning, which is clearly an essential first step towards becoming a professional translator. A lengthy recapitulation of social constructivism would not be appropriate here, particularly as there is an enormous amount of literature on Vygotsky's theory, much of it related to foreign language learning. I will assume that my readers are familiar with the various epistemologies that have played a paradigmatic role in the field of foreign language education over the past 100 years. But in a nutshell, social constructivism suggests that acquiring knowledge is not essentially the forming of habits (behaviourism), nor the result of an innate computational process (cognitivism), nor even a construction process that essentially occurs automatically within the heads of learners in the presence of suitable input (radical constructivism – based on Piaget's developmental psychology). Instead, from a social constructivist perspective, learning is understood to occur primarily as the result of pro-active communication through a synergistic co-construction process.

There are two closely related concepts that have been found to be of particular importance in understanding learning processes from a social constructivist perspective: Vygotsky's hypothesised *Zone of Proximal Development* (ZPD) and scaffolding. Vygotsky believed that an individual's true capability in a domain is better represented by what that person can do with help, rather than what he or she can do alone. Scaffolding then (actually a term coined by Jerome Bruner, but often used to refer to Vygotsky's learning theory) refers to the support offered by a teacher or a more knowledgeable peer during the learning process. Such support is most extensive early in a learning process and is withdrawn gradually as learners develop autonomy. The ZPD is the virtual space just beyond a learner's current level of competence where development occurs. In education, teachers with a social constructivist pedagogical epistemology will attempt to seek, create and take advantage of ZPDs as they appear, because those are the moments when learners are prepared to progress.

In the field of foreign language learning, the ZPD has sometimes been equated with Krashen's input hypothesis, which has also been called the i+1 or the comprehensible input hypothesis. The input hypothesis derives from the idea that language acquisition (that is: naturalistic learning) is the result of receiving, perceiving or taking in 'input' that is just slightly ahead of the current level of development. Although this might seem plausible on the surface, there are fundamental differences between the processes that these two perspectives propose as suggested in Dunn and Lantolf's (1998) article that investigated these differences and concluded that the two perspectives are incommensurable. From Krashen's perspective, acquisition occurs at a subconscious level when a learner is exposed to comprehensible input in which linguistic forms occur that are just slightly ahead of the learner's current level of competence in the foreign language. (Van Lier 2005: 138). From this perspective then, the process of learning is a largely automatic one as it is the mere presence of the next level of pre-programmed grammatical structures that stimulates and causes the 'acquisition' (accumulation) of those structures. The affective filter was proposed by Krashen to refer to the blockage that can occur in learning processes when learners experience stress. This is the reason for ensuring a comfortable, stress-free learning environment: to facilitate the automatic acquisition process. Epistemologically, this is a far cry from the hypothesised proactive, unpredictable and personalised nature of language development from a social constructivist perspective. In the words of Leo Van Lier, one of the pre-eminent proponents of an emergent view of language development and its application to teaching methodologies:

> In the i+1 condition, the learner might be a passive "loner", or at best an attentive receiver of the input coming her way. Nothing is assumed about co-construction, communities of practice, participation in cultural events, and so on. The ZPD on the other hand is created and driven by the activity of the learner, supported and guided by the more knowledgeable peer or teacher. In fact, without full and active participation by the learner, it is impossible to gauge exactly how to set in motion the proximal processes that will stimulate the capabilities that are in the process of developing. (Van Lier 2005: 155)

In comparing the disparate assumptions underlying the Natural Approach and a social constructivist approach to language acquisition, Van Lier depicts the radically different epistemologies that guide course designers and language teachers along two radically different paths. In Van Lier's (2005) words:

> i+1 assumes a transmissionist view of education, the ZPD a transformation view, the former adheres to the fixed code of an essentially monological language. The latter assumes an emergent, co-constructed dialogical language. As a result, the teacher in an I+1 context is a provider, someone who provides input, albeit while ensuring a positive affective climate, so that the input is not filtered out before entering the

learner's brain. The co-constructed dialogical language is no longer limited to approved bits of the standard language as prompted by textbooks and tests but it includes a variety of ways in which learners find their own voice. (p. 156)

The social constructivist epistemology, which, in my view represents the dominant paradigm in the field of foreign language teaching today, forms the axiomatic cornerstone of the SLE approach. This epistemology called for the 'B1 in nine months' project to utilise an approach that would be fundamentally different from both *SGAV* methodology and the *Natural Approach*, despite the fact that various holistic and humanistic features of both of those earlier approaches had a profound impact on my evolving understanding of the nature of language learning.

In this chapter, we have looked briefly at the concept of scaffolding as a suitable transmission alternative from a social constructivist epistemology to transmissionist teaching. In the next chapter, I would like to present the concept of emergence from a complexity thinking perspective as the second underlying principle of the scaffolded language emergence approach.

Chapter 5: A case for emergence as the key process underlying language learning

William Rutherford, whose numerous published works on grammar are held in high regard in the field of foreign language teaching, in setting the stage for an alternative, non-instructional, 'consciousness-raising' approach to the learning of grammar, echoed Werner Bleyhl when he wrote:

> A glance at any set of materials specifying grammatical information will usually reveal an inventory of syntactic constructs – e.g. relative clause, the present perfect, yes-no questions etc. And it is intended that these items should be directly 'taught' in some way in order that they be 'learned'. It is thus a matter of cutting up the target language into its putative constituent parts in order that the separate items may serve as units of pedagogical content, focus, practice, and eventual mastery. Language learning then, in other words, would seem to entail the steady accumulation of structural entities and language teaching would bring the entities to the learners' attention. (Rutherford 1987: 210)

Just as direct, deduction-based instruction has for a very long time been pervasively utilised within the language teaching community as a plausible technique for transmitting knowledge about a language and particularly its grammar in conventional classroom settings, Jerome Bruner's concept (1960, 1978) of scaffolding has been proposed and widely adopted as a plausible technique for fomenting learning from a transformational pedagogical perspective, where knowledge is understood to develop through iterative, dynamic, communicative interaction rather than through ingestion, repetitive practice, and accumulation. The principle that I believe exemplifies this transformative process is that of emergence. The theme of emergence suggests that a language, or more specifically, communicative competence in a language, cannot be taught, learned or acquired per se. All three terms suggest the transmission and accumulation of pieces of knowledge. Instead, from an emergence perspective, a language can be said and seen to grow and develop autopoietically within nested systems including individuals (and their many sub-systems, among them the physiological, psychological, cognitive and affective – to name but a few), dyads and groups of learners all the way up to entire language communities.

From the perspective of complexity thinking, all of these nested entities function as self-generating (autopoietic), self-regulating, adaptive systems. Complexity thinking, like complexity theory, has roots in the hard sciences but has also, over the last few decades, begun to be applied to a wide variety of domains, including the social sciences and education (See Finch 2001). Space in this little book does not permit anything more than a cursory discussion of the essence of the concept of emergence and its potential utility for foreign language learning, but the reader is encouraged to look at some of the many excellent works on complexity and emergence in various domains, including education in general, and second language acquisition studies specifically. (See, for example, Morçol 2001, Finch 2004 and Newell 2008). But while the themes of complexity and emergence have been investigated quite extensively over the past two decades with regard to second language acquisition, the only general language teaching approach that I am familiar with that seems to have been inspired by these themes is the Dogme approach mentioned in Chapter 1, and which, as I mentioned in that chapter would be an excellent approach to use in courses following introductory SLE courses.

In her pioneering article written 20 years ago that spurred research into the links between chaos theory, complexity science and second language acquisition, Diane Larsen-Freeman stated that, "there are many striking similarities between the new science of chaos/complexity and second language acquisition (SLA)" (1997: 141). Although she admitted that complexity theory may be of the greatest relevance in the physical sciences, Larsen-Freeman stated her conviction already at that early stage of her voluminous research in this domain that "the study of dynamic, complex nonlinear systems is meaningful in SLA" as well (ibid). As a result, she explored the nature of complex systems studied by complexity thinkers and demonstrated how a language can also be described as a dynamic, complex, nonlinear, unpredictable and self-organising system.

Complexity thinking is based on the belief that all manner of complex dynamic systems are 'emergent' in nature, that is: non-linear, unpredictable, self-generating and different from the sum of their parts. It is important to note that there is no single, monolithic domain called 'complexity theory'. Richardson & Cilliers (2001) have outlined a simple tripartite way to look at the study of complexity from three different perspectives: "a hard one, a soft one and something in between" (p. 5). The first is the perspective taken within hard sciences, like physics, with the objective of generating and testing theories that purport to explain the functioning of the physical world in mathematical terms[14]. The second – soft – perspective in complexity science is contrasted with the hard variety in that the former is applied to the study of social processes, for example, the nature of organisations. In Richardson and Cilliers' view, theories of complexity, which have primarily been developed through the study of natural, physical systems, cannot be directly applied to social systems (ibid). But from a 'soft' perspective, complexity theory is seen in terms of metaphorical tools. The third perspective is what Richardson and Cilliers call 'complexity thinking', which "focuses on the epistemological consequences of assuming the ubiquity of complexity." (ibid). While my post-positivist pedagogical epistemology has made me sceptical of the usefulness of applying positivist 'hard complexity theory' to the social domain, I believe that both soft complexity science and the third way, complexity thinking, can both be invaluable epistemological resources for understanding and fomenting foreign language learning.

In my view, if teachers see learning essentially as a linear process of accumulating knowledge initiated by instruction, and if we similarly see course design as a closed process, with each course having a finite beginning and an end based on teacher-specified objectives and content to be transmitted and assimilated in a uniform manner from individual to individual and from group to group, linearity is likely to be a self-fulfilling prophecy. That is, our courses will wind up as so many do: being closed-ended, controllable and excruciatingly predictable – and leading to the accumulation of more inert[15] than active knowledge. Alternatively, we can view the range of educational processes, from curriculum development through course design to activity creation, assessment and even educational research as part of a holistic ongoing process of life-long learning and action – with a potentially enormous array of often unexpected and fortuitously linked offshoots. Emergence, I suggest, is at the very least a potentially invaluable metaphor for transformational education – from individual learning through teacher training, down to the myriad design, development and implementation tasks that teachers are involved in day by day. I believe that we have a choice: either to cling to our long-held Cartesian beliefs in a fixed, perfectly knowable and controllable mechanical world, or to give up some of that control and in its place promote

---

14 Readers interested in 'hard' complexity theory applied to language may wish to consult MacWhinney and O'Grady's (2015) compendium of first-rate studies in this domain.
15 To borrow the term and concept from Alfred North Whitehead.

the self-organisation that increasingly appears to be characteristic of so many facets of our world – naturally, unpredictably and emergently (Larsen-Freeman 1997: 152).

This same dynamic view applies to language development itself, a term I prefer to 'acquisition' because the latter term suggests the input and intake of fixed structures from the environment (or a teacher). As such, (in contrast to the Chomskyan view and the principles of Krashen & Terrell's *Natural Approach)*, no innate language faculty is posited, even though, as indicated earlier, innate domain-general cognitive abilities and social drives may well exist. Instead, learners' language resources are thought to develop from interactions they experience and participate in.[16] This takes place through processes of co-adaptation (Larsen-Freeman & Cameron, 2008a) and 'soft assembly' – the dynamic process of constructing grammar as it is needed rather than consulting a registry of rules in long-term memory. Here we find a strong link between emergence and social constructivism, as Thelen & Smith (1994) outline in their seminal study:

> Language development itself occurs in social context. From a complexity theory perspective, such context contributes significantly to language development by affording possibilities for co-adaptation between interlocutors. As a learner interacts with another individual, their language resources are dynamically altered, as each adapts to the other – a mimetic process. [...] Co-adaptation is an iterative process; indeed, language development itself can be described as an iterative process, with learners visiting the same or similar territory repeatedly. (Thelen & Smith, 1994: 54)

Thelen and Smith (1994) coined the term 'soft-assembly' to refer to processes involving the manipulation and integration of multiple components of a system, where "each action is a response to the variable features of the particular task" (p. 64). Assembly is said to be 'soft' because the elements being assembled and the ways they are assembled are dynamic, changing at various points within a task and from one task to the next. From this perspective, collabora-

---

16 Of considerable interest here should be the work being done on the dialogical systems theory approach proposed by Karimi-Aghdam (2016). His view incorporates specifically the view that causality in L2 development is both bottom-up and top-down, a view that is intuitively plausible and on the surface at least seems to be very compatible with the complexity thinking underpinnings of SLE outlined here. This topic will be focused on in forthcoming publications.

tion among participants in a learning environment is absolutely essential and needs to be woven pervasively into learning activities – precisely the view supported by Vygotskian social constructivism.

Larsen-Freeman & Cameron (2008a) appropriated the term soft-assembly to refer to the way in which learners use their language resources to react to the communicative forces presented by their classmates and teachers. For L2 learners, these language resources include not only knowledge and skills they have learned with regard to the new language they are exploring, but their knowledge of their native and other previously learned languages as well, along with non-verbal communicative patterns. In the view of Thelen and Smith (1994), learners piece together the language that is emerging within them, taking into consideration the myriad sources of knowledge from their own personal histories, the contributions made by their interlocutors and the affordances of the contexts in which they find themselves.

The implications for classrooms in which complexity and emergence abound have been summarised concisely by Van Lier (1996), one of the most prominent, prolific and, in my view, convincing language education experts to have written on complexity, emergence and language learning:

> The educational context, with the classroom at its centre, is viewed as a complex system in which events do not occur in linear, causal fashion, but in which a multitude of forces interact in complex, self-organizing ways, and create changes and patterns that are part predictable, part unpredictable. (148)

Elsewhere, Van Lier emphasises the need for learners to be proactive seekers and makers of meaning and of the tools for meaning making. They cannot be passive recipients of ready-made knowledge:

> For language learning to occur we need access to the information in the environment. This information cannot just be transmitted to us, we must pick it up while being engaged in meaningful activities. That is […] we must first be active, then pick up language information that is useful for our activities. We may need assistance to be able to use and internalize the information, but we cannot just be passive vessels […] into which the information is poured. No, we must be engaged in activity and have information around that is available to be picked up and used. (Van Lier 2005: 97)

The classroom setting, the degree and type of preparation that facilitators (as opposed to instructors) will do prior to a class, the roles that participants will take during class sessions and the nature and intent of feedback provided will depend largely on the epistemological underpinnings of the approach adapted. The basic path for SLE at this point should be quite clear at this point:

> [...] the emergence perspective offers a potential framework and theoretical support for a rethinking of pedagogy that begins, not with a concept of pre-planned structure and hierarchy...but rather with the notion that the interaction of autonomous elements can lead to a productive, self-organizing structure. (Dalke et al.: 2007, p. 114)

On grammaticalisation: the emergence of grammar

The concept of grammaticalisation, or the process of creating one's own internal grammar in the context of language learning has been attributed to Rutherford (1987). As Van Lier (2005) points out, something akin to this process has long been a feature of second language acquisition studies, including in the comprehensible input hypothesis proposed by Steven Krashen. As Van Lier states:

> In that [Krashen's] view, just by being exposed to lots of comprehensible input, the learners will subconsciously acquire the complex structures of the language. In fact, Krashen argues, explicit teaching of grammar is virtually useless, since it only produces learned knowledge about language that is not usable in everyday communication. So, grammatical knowledge (or skill) develops automatically from listening to messages that are comprehensible. (ibid. p. 89)

As has already been discussed in Chapter 4, however, Krashen's innativist view suggests that the process of appropriating grammar is essentially a transmissionist one. Grammaticalisation proceeds apace as long as comprehensible input (i+1) is abundant in the learner's environment. Rather than functioning as a growing, emerging, nested network of nested systems that is involved in an interactive and synergistic creative process, from such a transmissionist view, the learning system is largely innate, mechanical, and accumulative.

From a complexity perspective, which is inherently non-innatist as it does not hypothesise an inborn Language Acquisition Device, the process of grammaticalisation is a pro-active construction process. From this viewpoint, in attempting to interact in authentic communicative situations, learners are actively engaged in a constant process of proposing and testing abductive hypotheses based on the myriad social, environmental, interpersonal, attitudinal, cognitive factors that converge in a given situation. From this perspective, much like the child learning its mother tongue, the non-infant learning an Ln in authentic, interesting and personally meaningful settings can be expected to piece the grammar together without a hypothetical Language Acquisition Device, but with the help of generic reasoning skills. Before moving on to Chapter 6, I would like to introduce the concept of 'affordance', which I have found to be of especial importance in re-assessing the role of 'input' in the learning process.

From input to affordances

The concept of 'input', used by Krashen to designate the linguistic material available to foreign language acquirers, has been discussed at some length already in Chapter 4. In concluding this chapter on emergence, however, I would like to return to the concept of input and outline briefly how I have found the term 'affordances,' coined by the psychologist James Gibson (1979), to be a far more appropriate and useful one than 'input' for understanding what students might be doing cognitively[17] while learning in a naturalistic environment (like an SLE classroom).

> An affordance is a particular property of the environment that is relevant – for good or for ill – to an active, perceiving organism in that environment. An affordance affords further action (but does not cause or trigger it). What becomes an affordance depends on what the organism does, what it wants and what is useful for it. (Van Lier 2000: 252)

This means that an affordance is not a property of either the learner or the environment, but of the relationship between the two. Affordances do not instruct: they offer, invite and solicit, they tempt, prod, contradict and elicit.

---

[17] When I use the term 'cognitive' here, I am using it in terms of a situated, embodied, holistic, and enactive process as it might be understood from the perspective of *situated cognition* (Brown et al. 1989).

They represent the wealth of opportunities in the environmental playground and laboratory that are the classroom.

Gibson's work actually focuses on mental processes in general rather than second language acquisition or foreign language learning, but his ideas have started to have an impact in educational domains as well. For Gifford, affordances are opportunities for interaction that exist in the environment relative to the sensory motor capacities of the animal. In other words, affordances are like options (or even invitations) for action offered by features of the environment in which a human being (or other animal) finds itself. To give an example of an affordance that comes up regularly in the first hour of our SLE classes at the FTSK, imagine a situation where the students have gathered in the classroom and are sitting on chairs arranged in a circle. The teacher (let's assume a teacher of English as a Second Language) at some point (usually after a very brief introduction) dives into a *Total Physical Response* activity during which the learners will be introduced to the names for a number of items in the classroom and verbs of action that might collocate with those items. The facilitator might stand up and say "I am standing up". She might then sit down, saying at the same time, "I am sitting down", and so on. She might move around the room naming items in English and accompanying her words with gestures and actions. She might then invite the students to "Sit down on your chairs", without having said "I am sitting down on my chair" while presenting the items and actions. The students will invariably understand the meaning of "on" because of the generic affordance provided by a chair. Chairs are meant to be sat upon. None of the words will have been translated for the learners during the presentation phase, so they will all be dependent on taking advantage of the affordances offered by the facilitator's gestures and by the structure and normal uses of items touched or pointed at during the activity. Van Lier, one of most outspoken foreign language learning scholars in writing about the value of affordances, has said[18]:

> From an ecological perspective, the learner is immersed in an environment full of potential meanings. These meanings become available gradually as the learner acts and interacts within and with this environment. Learning is not ... a piecemeal migration of meanings to the inside of the learner's head, but rather the development of increasingly effective ways of dealing with the world and its meanings. (Van Lier 2000: 246)

---

18 He has also been one of the most eloquent, which is why I have quoted him here at some length.

To my mind, this represents a clear break with the conventional transmissionist view of the learning process. From this perspective, learners engage with affordances they perceive and often seek out in their environment (rather than mere input).

> The linguistic world to which the learner has access, and in which she becomes actively engaged, is 'full of demands and requirements, opportunities and limitations, rejections and invitations, enablements and constraints – in short, affordances.' (Shorter and Newson 1982: 34) quoted in Van Lier 2000, p. 253.

This shift from understanding the process of learning as one of entailing the taking in of input to one of negotiating meaning with others in a rich social, material and experiential environment changes the roles that both learners and teachers assume in the learning process. To express the underlying theme of this book and the SLE approach once again in slightly different terms: language can be understood to emerge within the context of dealing with affordances of the environment on the one hand and negotiating meaning with one's peers and facilitators on the other:

> [...] in negotiating meaning, a piece of language that was not comprehensible before, now becomes comprehensible as a result of negotiation work and can thus be incorporated into the learner's target-language repertoire. (ibid: 247)

This view of language learning as entailing a dynamic, pro-active and negotiated process of meaning making elucidates the need for a radical shift from the carefully prescribed and restricted linguistic syllabus underlying *All's Well* and the seemingly mechanical feeding of the Language Acquisition Device in the *Natural Approach* to a far more open-ended and authentic learning process in the SLE approach. Van Lier's (2000) explanation of the learning process in terms of semiotic activity provides a particularly vivid and germane perspective on the learning processes as I see them in SLE classes:

> In terms of learning, language emerges out of semiotic activity. The context is not just there to provide input (linguistics models or objects) to a passive recipient. The environment provides a "semiotic budget" (analogous to the energy budget of an ecosystem) within which the active

learner engages in meaning-making activities together with others, who may be more, equally or less competent in linguistic terms. The semiotic budget does not refer to the amount of 'input' available, nor the amount of input that is enhanced for comprehension, but to the opportunities for meaningful action that the situation affords. (252)

In winding up this very brief but, I believe, important discussion of affordances, and in bringing this chapter to a close, I offer the latest version of my model of language learning (L1, L2....Ln) in Figure 1. In this minimalist model, which I have presented in several rather different configurations to depict the development of translator competence (see, for example, Kiraly 2015), I have attempted to include only the most salient factors that I have so far managed to identify in a language emergence environment. I have given the model the form of a vortex to emphasise that what is being depicted is a pervasively dynamic, non-linear view of language development. There are no inputs and no outcomes indicated in the model, because the process from my perspective is an organic and autopoietic (self-generating and self-maintaining) one that relies on affordances (opportunities for action) and signifiers (cues to enable us to function in our complex world) (Norman 2008; 18). Donald Norman, an expert in the field of design, proposed the term signifier to augment that of affordance, which he felt was too limited. For Norman, a signifier can be understood as an affordance that be interpreted, that is, one that offers or carries meaning, either intentionally or unintentionally. An affordance, on the other hand, invites the perceiver to act because of some specific properties it has. I am very intrigued by Norman's addition to this discussion, but I have addressed it in this volume only superficially. A more in-depth consideration of the implications for SLE will have to wait for a later publication.

Returning to the model, we can see, spiralling up around the vortex, intertwined ribbons of constraints and opportunity that are intended to reflect Jerome Bruner's concept of 'scaffolding' – in this context, the support provided by the environment for the emergence of communicative competence. In this model, scaffolding is seen as being provided by the various dispositions, affordances that impact the emergence of language, and that facilitators can focus on and work with in co-constructing a rich environment in which a new language can begin to emerge.

So far, I have identified four basic groups of features that I believe are fundamental to naturalistic language learning. (These, too, are abductive hypotheses). These features will be discussed in more detail in Chapter 6, which summarises the theoretical concepts presented in this first section of the book and provides guidance for teachers who wish to create their own SLE courses. Many of these features will also reappear in Section II of the book, where they will be situated in actual classroom activities that have been created and implemented by student facilitators in our various SLE language courses at the FTSK in recent years.

A Model of Emergent Language Learning

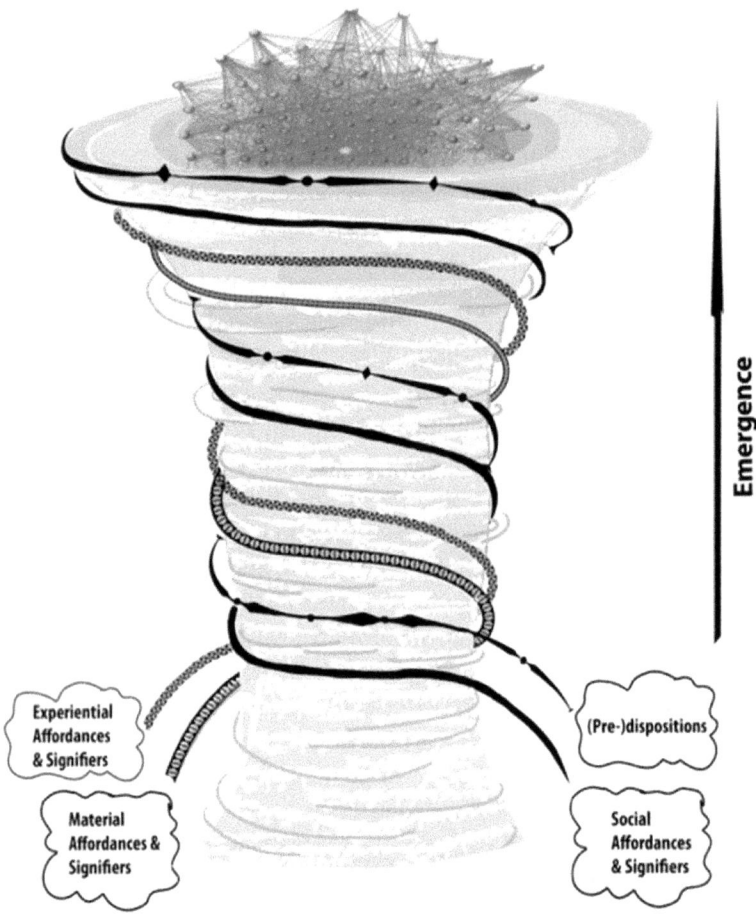

Figure 1: Language Learning Seen as an Emergent Process

Dispositions, Affordances and Signifiers

1. **Personal (pre-) dispositions** (including prior knowledge as well attitudes that students bring with them to the course, and the readiness and willingness to participate in course activities – which may, of course, vary from one class to the next).

2. **Experiential affordances and signifiers** (links between an individual and aspects of the environment that one experiences through action – like pedagogical tasks and activities, and communicative interaction between facilitators and learners as well as among learners).

3. **Material affordances and signifiers** (concrete features of and objects in the environment that can contribute to the conveyance or emergence of meaning). These may include relations to objects to be found in virtually any classroom as well as to realia that the facilitators and learners may bring into the learning environment during a course.

4. **Social signifiers** (ideational and cultural artefacts in the learning environment that can contribute to the conveyance or emergence of meaning)

Chapter 6: Pedagogical beacons

This final chapter of the theoretical section of this book has the objective of bringing together the disparate ideas, concepts, epiphanies and findings presented up to this point in the form of a set of pedagogical beacons for would-be SLE facilitators. These are the abductively derived principles that guide my own course design and facilitating praxis and that I have tried to share with every new team of student-facilitators that I have worked with. This is the first time that they are appearing in written form and it is inevitable that after further reflection on and experimentation with the approach, revisions will be forthcoming. In any event, from a complexity perspective, it is essential in my view to see the approach itself as an emergent entity that will continue to develop over time. Its viability will in fact depend on its dynamism. It is important to keep in mind that the assumptions and pedagogical beacons presented here are my own and in no way fixed in stone. I use them as reminders for myself and as suggestions for prospective SLE facilitators, and even though they may be phrased as if they were fixed guidelines, there is no implied rule-like quality to any of these suggestions. They are to be seen only as reminders of key features of the approach as I have envisaged it up to this point.

Underlying Assumptions	Pedagogical Beacons
1. Affordances and signifiers rather than input are the primary stimuli for learning	Focus on affordances rather than trying to provide input
2. Knowledge is often socially constructed	Promote autonomy and collaboration, provide scaffolding
3. Perceived authenticity aids motivation and learning	Seek authenticity and encourage authentication
4. Affect is a key factor in learning	Welcome affect into the classroom
5. Language is embodied	Focus on corporeal connections
6. Grammaticalisation depends on induction and abduction	Emphasise inductive-abductive reasoning
7. Linearity constrains learning	Welcome complexity

Table 1: The assumptions underlying the SLE approach and derived pedagogical beacons

I. **Facilitators focus more on working with affordances and on the basis of learners (pre)dispositions than on providing input**

If we as language teachers and learners take the perspective that a language develops autopoietically as a dynamic system rather than being an accumulation of bits of that language taken in from input, I suggest that we clearly must move away from an input/intake view of the teaching/learning process towards a scaffolding/emergence view. What the SLE approach proposes is that facilitators (whose roles include guiding, supporting, encouraging and nudging the natural processes of emergence in each individual and in the group as a whole) need to look to experiential, material and social affordances (or signifiers) as their primary tools for enabling naturalistic learning processes to proceed. Input would be a sensible metaphor if we were to see language as a collection of linguistic items and rules, and the learner essentially as a computer, with the ability to apply programmed rules in a largely mechanical manner but without social, embodied and emotional (i.e. visceral) capabilities that are essential facets of what makes us human.[19]

At the same time, we must of course always be aware of each student's unique constellation of pre-dispositions (language learning aptitude, previous experience learning foreign languages, intrinsic and extrinsic motivation for learning the Ln and personality factors), and dispositions (willingness to engage deeply in particular learning activities, and willingness to learn collaboratively, willingness to accept the course implementer as a guide, mentor and partner rather than an instructor and controller). The facilitator's focus shifts clearly towards the learners individually and as a learning community, and towards the learning environment, which in the end is the playing field, the laboratory and the microcosm that serves as the fertile greenhouse in which a new language can emerge. The facilitators' (near) native speaker competence is of course an absolutely essential component of the environment, providing extensive natural contact to the language that is to emerge as the lingua franca of the group that presumably will have come together for the express purpose of fomenting precisely this emergence. But the providing of input becomes a moot point once we leave behind transmissionist metaphors for what goes on in our SLE classrooms:

---

[19] Readers who would like guidance specifically on 'facilitating' are encouraged to consult Adrian Underhill's article (1999) entitled: "Facilitation in language teaching".

In an interactive system, the teacher's primary task is not to conceive and implement organisation de novo, or in isolation from other participants in the classroom. Instead, the teacher's distinctive role is to create the kind of rich environment within which productive organisation can emerge from the interactions of all participants. (Dalke et al. 2007: p. 114)

II. It is essential for facilitators to promote both autonomy and peer collaboration, and to provide scaffolding

Peer collaboration

For Vygotsky, participation in genuine communicative situations is the basis for intellectual development. From the perspective of the SLE approach, authentic communication provides learners with the same kinds of exploratory and problem-solving work to promote the emergence of a foreign language as has been identified in the learning of one's native tongue. As we are not dealing with input and an innate system for importing a pre-existing system, SLE focuses instead on inductive learning, abductive thinking and hypothesis testing that can be applied in the negotiation of meaning that is endemic in authentic communication within a community of peers – and that can be guided and supported by facilitators who are fluent in the Ln. Learning, and particularly the learning of a language, is neither a spectator sport nor a task that learners undertake individually. From Vygotsky's perspective, it is communicative action that precedes thought and language, and not the other way around. Learners need to interact and in so doing, use language, which gradually emerges into a complex tool that can be used in a wide range of communicative settings.

Autonomy

While peer collaboration is an essential ingredient in language emergence in the classroom, the ever-increasing autonomy of learners also needs to be emphasised from the beginning of a course through the end. While learners are dependent on extensive scaffolding at the beginning of an initiatory course, they must increasingly become autonomously competent in using the Ln as they progress, and they must also become more and more autonomous as learners, given that courses will be of relatively short duration but learning goes on for a lifetime. Autonomy has been proposed, along with communicative competence, as one of the two key emergent outcomes of SLE-based courses:

> [...] as learners move up the academic ladder, they increasingly have to work on their own to study independently for periods of time. One might say that in a sense they internalize previously encountered teaching practices as well as social reasoning processes, and become their own "virtual teacher", as it were. They manage and focus their attention, they select and act upon the affordances they themselves located in the study environment, and engage in inner instructional dialogue. (Van Lier: 2005, p. 157)

Scaffolding

Scaffolding involves the providing of stimuli, support and feedback that nudge and guide each learner and the group as a whole from the beginning of a course to the end. This is the facilitator's primary role:

> The teacher has the [...] task of encouraging, facilitating and nudging the process of emergence, of helping to assure that it evolves in directions that are engaging and productive for all. (ibid., p. 162).

Scaffolding, however, is not a one-way street. It also involves the constant observation of and gathering of information about the dynamic learning environment, ongoing negotiation with the learners, and the spontaneous adjustment of support to promote learner autonomy and competence. The facilitator's efforts are scaffolded by the learner' actions, by the language they can understand and produce at any given moment from the beginning of a course to the end. While facilitators will surely have a general plan for guiding and accompanying the learners from almost zero communicative competence in the Ln to a solid rudimentary competence upon which they can continue to build, facilitators must always remain open to and must respond to their learners' epiphanies, setbacks and queries. To borrow from and extend the well-known image depicted by Antonio Machado and Paolo Freire, facilitators and learners in an SLE environment (including children learning their mother tongue and their interlocutors) create the path to a new language path by walking it. In this process, scaffolding is not so much a technique as a communicative style, based on empathy and intuitive facilitating efficacy:

> The complexity and selection of tasks, and the design of options for different students, depend to a large extent on how well the teacher understands the students. This is another reason why pedagogical scaffolding is beneficial for teachers: it requires constant watching and monitoring of student activity, and therefore fosters an understanding of the student's interests and abilities. (ibid., p. 207)

III. Seek authenticity and encourage authentication in the classroom

Authenticity has been a prominent topic of interest in language teaching literature for close to 40 years. Widdowson (1979) is attributed with having identified a valuable distinction between genuine and authentic language use. In his view, a bit of realia brought into the classroom or an activity based on real communicative interaction in the Ln can be considered genuine, but authenticity refers to a relationship between that material or activity and the learner. An authentic use of a newspaper article might be to have learners read it for comprehension or as background information for a debate. Having learners memorise the text or fill in every nth deleted word in a cloze exercise would presumably be inauthentic, as it would not have anything to do with genuine, non-pedagogical communication. As Van Lier (1996), who picked up on Widdowson's initial conceptualisation and advanced the discussion revolving around 'authenticity' stated:

> [...] it is easy to bring genuine pieces of language into the classroom, but to create authentic opportunities of language use on their basis appears to be quite another matter. As Widdowson points out, genuine texts must be authenticated by the learners, but the conditions for authentication are hard to pinpoint. (p. 126)

Both Widdowson and Van Lier refer to the concept of 'authentication' which entails taking a stance towards a text or activity in the class and dealing with it in an authentic way.

[...] authenticity is not brought into the classroom with the materials or the lesson plan, rather, it is a goal that teachers and students have to work towards, consciously and constantly. [...] authenticity is the result of acts of authentication, by students and their teacher, of the learning process and the language used in it. The teacher may be instrumental in promoting authenticity, although this may be a lot easier to achieve in some settings, and students, than in others. (ibid.)

Van Lier points out that conventional exercises can also be considered authentic in that teachers (who are more knowledgeable about the language and whose job it is ostensibly to help learners acquire it) traditionally instruct learners, that is teach them about the language. Both Steven Krashen (1982) and Michel Paradis (2009) have argued convincingly that the overt teaching of formal linguistic rules has as little place in a natural language development scenario as repetitive drills, overt correction or testing for the memorisation of linguistic structures. From a social constructivist perspective, the Ln is structured by the individual through interaction with others on the basis of intuition and feel; the language becomes part of the learner as the learner becomes part of the language community. And from an emergentist perspective, a grammar emerges in each individual through communicative interaction in the respective language.

On the basis of this line of reasoning, in the SLE courses we have run at the FTSK, we have consistently focused on maximising genuine communication in the classroom and have proposed that a supplementary session be offered at the end of each class day (or as needed), where learners and facilitators can focus specifically on form, where everyone can speak in the learners' mother tongue, and where teachers can function as teachers if they wish and if this is desired by the learners. During regular class sessions, however, there is no use of the learners' native tongue, activities take the form of all sorts of communicative activities, including role play, sketches, creative work and games. But conventional language exercises focused essentially on providing, practicing and testing linguistic input and intake are relegated to the after-hours sessions.

In *A Social Constructivist Approach to Translator Education* (Kiraly 2000: 42-44), I advocated a 'situated learning' approach, by analogy with *situated cognition*, which goes beyond embodied cognition in acknowledging the multifarious ways (social, biological, interactive and personal) in which learning is anchored in the life and the world beyond the brain. Scott Thornbury (2013), one of the two creators of the SLE-like Dogme approach (mentioned in the introduction to this volume), describes his situated view as an 'ecological' one, encompassing the realisation that cognition is "physically embodied, embedded in its situational context, and that its reach extends beyond the biological brain". (p. 72) In emphasising physical embodiment, Thornbury notes specifically the value of the *Total Physical Response* technique, "which exploits the physical nature of the classroom ecology". He echoes Earl Stevick's (1996: 132) support for TPR:

> [...] it encourages – indeed, practically forces – multi-sensory involvement and resulting multi-sensory images… It meets in an integrated way needs that are physical and social as well as cognitive. (Quoted in Thornbury (2013: p. 64).

IV. Facilitators welcome affect in the classroom

Taking into account the affective facet of learners' holistic selves has been a recurrent theme in so-called 'alternative' approaches and methods for foreign language learning. Steven Krashen's hypothesised 'affective filter', which he suggested needed to be kept low to ensure unfettered intake of linguistic input, is perhaps the best-known explicit reference to the role of affect in Ln learning. In the introduction to her insightful edited volume, appropriately entitled *Affect in Language Learning,* Arnold (1999) outlined the breadth of the affective terrain that has been the focus of attention in the fields of second language acquisition and foreign language learning[20]. The holistic epistemological foundation of SLE encourages the course designer and facilitator to take into account the many facets of learners, learning environments, and interpersonal relations within the emergent classroom setting. In terms of affect, they will need to consider such aspects as: empathy, anxiety, inhibitions, extroversion/introversion, self-esteem, extrinsic and intrinsic motivation, learner styles, classroom transactional styles and cross-cultural processes. (ibid).

This is not to suggest that conventional teachers will not take these aspects into account, but rather that a highly interactive, embodied and socially dy-

---

[20] Readers interested in delving further into research on this topic are encouraged to consult the broad range of sub-topics covered in *Affect in Language Learning* (Arnold 1999).

namic SLE classroom will allow these affective factors to come to the surface, whereas in a chalk-and-talk environment, the affective dimension of learners (and facilitators) can and is very likely to be radically restricted. Along with raising their own awareness of these factors by consulting reference works like Arnold (1999), would-be facilitators are encouraged to discuss affective factors and how they can be dealt with while working in teams to create courses, and to exchange feedback on each other's interactions in the classroom. In my view, the key to mastering affective factors in the SLE classroom is being aware of one's own empathy towards the other participants in the learning environment. As the control-related roles of facilitators fade into the background behind roles like that of guide, assistant and facilitator, I have found that affective problems tend to take care of themselves. Clearly, for reasons related to empathy and the desire to control outcomes, for example, an excellent teacher may not make an outstanding facilitator. It will be up to would-be facilitators to decide for themselves to what extent they feel comfortable in a facilitating role.

V. A focus on corporeal connections encourages naturalistic, whole-person learning

Approaches, methods and techniques including the *Natural Approach*, *SGAV*, and *Total Physical Response* have provided us with excellent examples of how language can be seen to be embodied and how we can effectively incorporate learners' corporeal selves into the learning process. In the field of Second Language Acquisition Studies, the first generation cognitivist paradigm dating back to Noam Chomsky's invention of transformational grammar and the 'mind-as-computer' metaphor shifted to a network-type metaphor and connectionism in the 1980s, but has since been overshadowed by the emerging new paradigm that has been called 'second-generation cognitive science' (Lakoff & Johnson 1999). From this perspective, cognition is not confined to the individual brain, but can be situated in the individual's body and corporeal functions (embodied) and also distributed in the environment (extended).

Hanna Risku, who has been applying complexity thinking in her research on Translation Studies and Technical Communication for at least 20 years, has summarised succinctly the embodied cognition perspective which readers are encouraged to investigate further in the wealth of literature that has been produced on this alternative to seeing cognition solely as an intracranial biological process:

> The primary concern of situated, embodied cognition is the fact that individual history and the present environment form an integral part of the processes of thought and behaviour. Therefore, thought cannot be localized in the brain, even though the brain plays a major role: we also think by carrying out physical, epistemic actions, ordering and reordering the environment and changing our focus of perception and attention through eye and body movements in order to simplify or alter the problems confronted. According to situated, embodied cognition, perception does not produce internal images, and action is not dependent on cognitive plans and maps. (Risku 2010: p. 98).

For SLE facilitators, adopting a holistic, embodied view of cognition (and hence learning) clearly adds a component of complexity to course and activity planning, but it also harkens back to what parents, caretakers and older siblings do automatically when dealing with babies and small children in whom the native tongue is emerging: they play, role-play, and interact in myriad embodied ways with them. Not only does embedding inter(action) in 'action' support memory for words and linguistic patterns, it also uncovers and utilises social, material and experiential affordances that are part and parcel of meaning-making. Once teachers leave behind the idea that language structure can and must primarily be 'taught' overtly (and primarily deductively), drawing on embodied cognitive action in the classroom is sure to come naturally, as it appears to have done for the many student-facilitators who have created their own SLE courses at the FTSK. Readers are encouraged to look for examples of embodied action in Sarah Signer's practical section of this book in which various aspects of a number of our courses are depicted.

VI. Inductive-abductive reasoning leads to grammaticalisation

The idea that the structure of a language can emerge without the memorisation of an extensive set of rules and without countless repetitive exercises may well appear implausible if not absurd against the backdrop of conventional scholastic language teaching principles. And yet, some prominent language education scholars disagree:

[...] it is not necessary to posit a central, rule-governed, mental grammar functioning in a top-down manner. The knowledge underlying fluent, systematic, apparently rule-governed language use is the learner's entire collection of memories of previously experienced utterances, both the learner's own and those attended to in co-adapting to interlocutors. (Larsen-Freeman, 2011: 55)

There is, in fact, considerable evidence that grammar is generated (or emerges) within each individual as the result of creative social and cognitive processes:

Grammaticalisation is basically the idea that the acquisition of grammar (or in more general terms, the formal complexities of the language, which are mainly phonological and morpho-syntactic) occurs not as a result of an accumulation of explicitly learned rules, but rather as the result of cognitive and/or social activity using the language in meaningful ways [...]. In L1 acquisition, grammaticalisation is well documented as a non-linear example of emergence. (ibid.)

The concept of the Emergent Grammar dates back almost 20 years to when Hopper (1998) formulated it much as I understand it today against the background of more than a decade of work with the concept in the context of our SLE courses at the FTSK:

The notion of Emergent Grammar is meant to suggest that structure, or regularity, comes out of discourse and is shaped by discourse as much as it shapes discourse in an on-going process. Grammar is hence not to be understood as a pre-requisite for discourse, a prior possession attributable in identical form to both speaker and hearer. Its forms are not fixed templates, but are negotiable in face-to-face interaction in ways that reflect the individual speakers' past experience of these forms, and their assessment of the present context, including especially their interlocutors, whose experiences and assessments may be quite different. Moreover, the term Emergent Grammar points to a grammar which is not abstractly formulated and abstractly represented, but always anchored in the specific concrete form of an utterance. (Hopper 1998: p. 142)

Like virtually everything else in an SLE environment, error correction is also seen as a naturalistic process involving facilitating more than instructing. Instead of interrupting the students' discourse when a linguistic error is heard in an effort to nip incipient faults in the bud, facilitators provide proleptic feedback, which is more of an offer of unobtrusive constructive support geared to help learners to reflect on and reassess the communicative plausibility or even accuracy of their utterances and the validity of their evolving hypotheses about how the new language functions. In the absence of deductively learned rules in the initial stages of our courses, acquirers' minds can work constantly to make sense of and restructure the new communicative system using their panoply of already well-developed conceptual tools and interactional skills. In the second section of this book, readers will find examples of proleptic feedback that have been observed in FTSK courses.

VII. It is essential to welcome complexity in the classroom

Learners become active (pro-active and co-active) participants in SLE courses. Instead of having a rigid progression of linguistic structures imposed on them by teachers using the conventional techniques of repetitive exercises and unnatural dialogues (in which teachers persistently ask questions the answers to which they already know, and in this way distort the concept of a mutually synergistic dialogue, turning it into a pseudo-communicative exercise), are replaced with largely open-ended situations where the learners can bring in their own interests, areas of expertise, curiosity and personal goals. The key here, I believe, is to leave room for unexpected turns of events – keeping the students (and facilitators!) in a state of anticipation. This reflects the spontaneity inherent in unscripted first language acquisition.

The learning agenda for each SLE course emerges in an ongoing, dynamic manner as each group interacts with its facilitators, the learning activities they undertake together, and the affordances in the learning environment. Instead of breaking down the linguistic system of a language for transfer to and ingestion by the learners, the facilitators actively seek ways to work with these affordances in order to instigate natural emergence and eventually autonomous learning.

From this perspective, more suitable (and abductively derived) categories than frequency in discourse have emerged to scaffold pedagogical progression in our SLE courses. They include:

- Progressing from the here-and-now to what came before, to what will be and then what might be and might have been – with appropriate linguistic structures appearing in the ambient language as needed,
- Starting with situations encouraging a focus on relationships between the self and the world, then moving on to dyadic relations, then on to the inside group (we), and then to the outside group (they) – rather than practising verb conjugations, for example, which are notoriously absent from natural communication,
- Moving from the concrete to the abstract,
- Progressing from comprehension to situated production.

This sort of dynamic organising structure can be applied recursively, not only as part of the framework for a curriculum for a year's program of study, but also for the syllabus of a single intensive course, a week of classes, and the activities for a given day or hour. This way of looking at progression also reflects the progression in the psychological development of the child, providing the approach with a naturalistic set of categories that reflect other aspects of human life and our own communicative development in our native tongues.

The activities developed by the teachers revolve around a set of themes that are chosen intuitively as ones that would facilitate multi-modal communication and reflect common if not universal topics of interest to beginning adult language students. Themes used during our intensive SLE courses have included: family, travel, food and cooking, hobbies, furniture, shopping, sports, clothing and professions. Activities involving food and cooking, for example, have included: 1) having students bring in food items to make breakfast together 2) selecting recipes from the respective country and preparing the corresponding dishes in the school's kitchen; visiting a local fruit and vegetable merchant to learn the names of foods and 3) taking a trip to the grocery store to purchase items needed for the preparation of a joint meal.

In any event, there are no fixed or generic syllabi for SLE courses. Acknowledging the complexity of the classroom means embracing it. Facilitators need to learn to initiate emergence, helping students to bootstrap themselves into elementary communicative competence in the Ln. They then need to move on to help the learners expand their competence and their independence as users and learners of their new language. This process should always revolve around empathy, negotiation and the learners' needs and interests. Over the past decade of use and continued development of the SLE approach at the FTSK, we have seen that communicative competence and communicative as well as learning autonomy and a sense of empowerment appear to be self-evident outcomes, at least for our highly motivated and communicatively adroit students.

There is thus no easy answer to the need for adjusting the complexity level of tasks to learners' abilities. The more students can participate in the design, and the more they can feel in charge, experience ownership, have a sense of being in control of their own actions, the more likely it is that students will be engaged, that they will be intrinsically motivated, and that they will make choices that are in the best interest of their language development. (Van Lier 1996: p. 207)

Moving on from theory to practice

This brings us to the end of the more theoretical section of this introduction to the SLE approach to elementary foreign language learning. In the second section, Sarah Signer will present the approach from its more practical side. She has gathered, organised and interpreted findings from seven BA and MA theses which have been written about various SLE courses that have been offered at the FTSK over the past decade. Our intention is for this section to provide some insight into how SLE courses and activities look in practice.

To summarise the theoretical aspects covered in this section, I have included the graphic depiction presented in Figure 2 below. The figure covers three main aspects of the SLE approach: the underlying assumptions; course design beacons; and plausible emergent outcomes. The seven underlying assumptions are reflected in the seven course design beacons. And I have subsumed the many possible outcomes of SLE courses under just two categories: autonomy and competence. By autonomy, I mean both the ability of learners to function more or less successfully in situations where the emergent language is the lingua franca of the interlocutors, as well as the capability for continued (even life-long) learning after the SLE course is over. As for competence, I am thinking essentially of elementary communicative competence in all its facets.

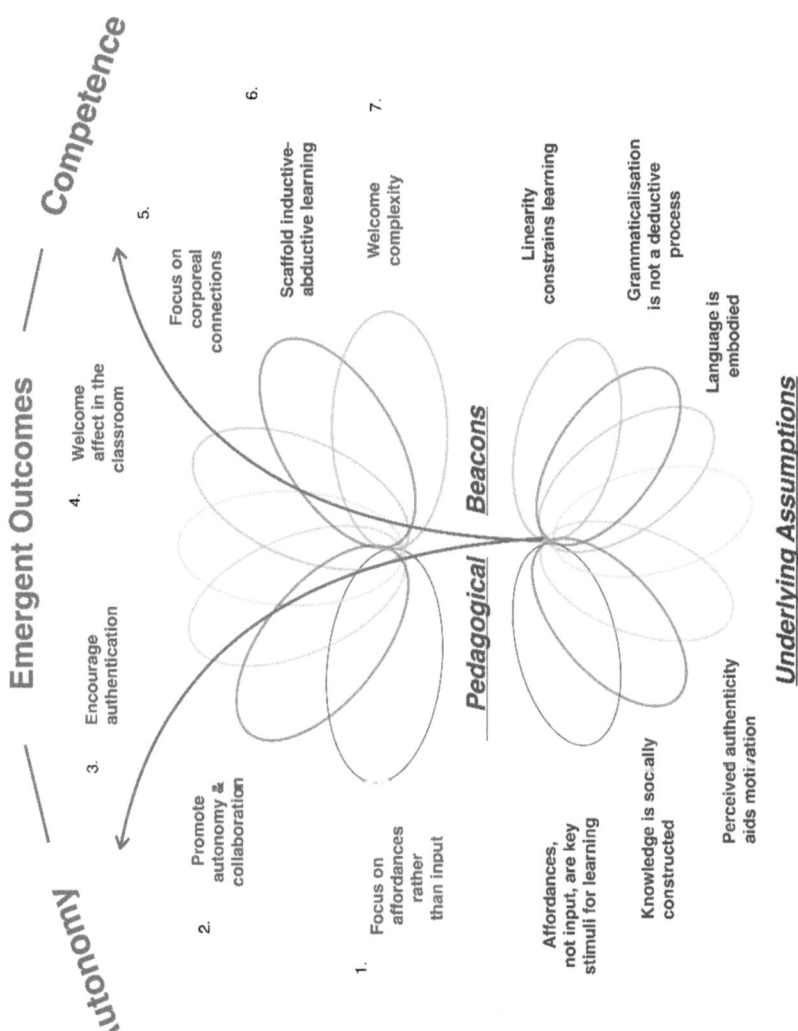

Figure 2: SLE Assumptions, Beacons and Outcomes

SARAH SIGNER

SECTION II: FROM THEORY TO EXEMPLARY PRACTICE

Introduction

The second section of this book provides authentic examples of how the theory described in the first section has been implemented in a number of foreign language courses at the FTSK over the past decade. The main focus is on the learners and facilitators, and includes instances of both their success and their moments of frustration, the innovative learning environments and creative activities that were developed as well as comparisons between Scaffolded Language Emergence (SLE) courses and more traditional ways of promoting learning. The section is divided into five chapters. The classroom examples are instantiated with original information gleaned from theses written by FTSK students. Even though this approach can only be understood well by considering the individual components as integral to the whole, segregating the various examples in distinct chapters seemed necessary for ensuring as reader-friendly a presentation as possible.

When Don broached the idea of co-authoring this book and asked me to contribute a collection of examples to illustrate the various aspects encompassed by the approach, I was initially somewhat hesitant as I have never participated in an SLE course either as a learner or a facilitator. All I would have to go on were a number of BA and MA theses written about the courses by students in the Division of English Linguistics and Translation Studies at the FTSK. Fortunately, the quality of these theses is very good, and more importantly, they include many relevant examples of affordances and signifiers as well as direct quotes from the learners and facilitators, so my initial reservations dissipated quickly. This section should provide the reader with a fairly balanced – but of course still subjective – account of what they might expect from applying an SLE approach in the classroom. Please note that the radical difference in organisational structure between the two sections of the book was intentional. Our objective was to provide two rather different accounts of SLE processes: one more theoretical and one more practical, but without attempting to structure the two sections in the same way. We hope that this decision is in our readers' interest.

All names of the facilitators and learners quoted in this section have been changed to preserve their anonymity.

Chapter 7: Affordances, signifiers and embodiment in the SLE classroom

The first chapter of this section deals with affordances and signifiers in the learning environment and the embodiment of language in SLE classrooms at the FTSK. Affordances or signifiers refer to the cues for action offered by objects, experiences and social relations that learners are confronted with during collaborative activities but that can be experienced differently in terms of the opportunities they offer. The examples presented in this chapter provide implicit suggestions on how to work with affordances to cater to the learners' wide range of dispositions and predispositions. Embodiment is a fundamental element of dealing with these affordances that promotes the authentication of activities undertaken in SLE classes.

The initial focus in this chapter is on a discussion of the in-class use of sketches (brief scenes acted out by the facilitators in class) within the SLE approach, their purpose, and the advantages they can provide for both facilitators and learners. In a number of the courses taught at the FTSK, the facilitators have decided to introduce new vocabulary by acting out various sketches for the students using either a script or conversation notes and prompts. One of the primary benefits of using sketches is that unknown words can be 'experienced' by the learner in a quasi-natural setting. They allow facilitators to focus on what they feel to be useful and pertinent basic vocabulary and expressions to help the learners bootstrap themselves into each new topic while, at the same time, scaffolding the situation according to the learners' needs. A further advantage of sketches in a classroom setting is that both facilitators and learners can add in corporeal components of meaning with the help of gestures and movement to stimulate deeper understanding. If the student learns to associate a movement or gesture with a specific word, seeing or performing the respective gesture or movement can be expected to trigger the term in the learner's mind.

When activities also involve the learners rather than only the facilitators, a sketch is more commonly referred to as 'role-playing' and ultimately serves the same purpose. It enables the students to move from authenticated semi-communicative situations to genuine communication but does not preclude alternating between activities involving simulated and real communication:

> In order to recreate realistic situations in which language is used naturally, we implemented mainly role-playing activities that aimed to shift the focus from the simulation of real communication to genuine communication. (Rizzo, p. 18)

While role-playing frequently provides the learners with opportunities to move and use their bodies while using the Ln, it has been noticed in our SLE courses that some learners will struggle to act or move naturally while they are speaking in a foreign language. Therefore, the facilitators in the FTSK courses also use additional action-inducing techniques, such as games that actively emphasise movement or activities that focus on familiar operations (e.g., shopping, cooking, consulting a doctor), to ensure that learners engage their bodies as well as their minds in the language emergence process.

The data collected from the learners indicates that passive learning through mere observation often does not have the desired effect, i.e. it often does not provide them with an adequate basis for remembering new words. In the post-course surveys, some students have even expressed an active dislike for passive learning situations:

> I was following this scene passively, trying to connect words with meanings. For a short-time, I could remember them. But just a couple of minutes later, I could not produce a single word. (Julia, in Buring, p. 53)

and

> Today, I honestly had to ask 30 times how you say 'cup' […]. I had thought I would be able to remember it. However, this was simply not the case. (Sebastian, in Buring, p. 65)

or

> I didn't like the activity because we only sat there and listened to what [the teachers] said! (Katharina, in Destreel, p. 57)

A technique employed in many SLE classrooms is James Asher's *Total Physical Response* (TPR). As the following quote shows, some learners consider movement, particularly in the form of gestures, to be beneficial to the development of their language skills; one student mentioned the advantages of using her hands during communicative situations: "I make a gesture and then there is an immediate 'click' in my mind and I know the [...] word" (Silvia, in Buring, p. 54). However, activities involving TPR will not automatically lead to the desired outcome if they are not situated effectively or connected to meaning, that is, if students do not understand why they are being asked to move and follow commands. Following a TPR activity that was disconcerting because it was not linked in any clear way to the previous situation that the class had been dealing with, one student commented: "I did not quite get what the activity was good for" (Tobias, in Destreel, p. 33). This sentiment was shared by a large portion of the group and required the facilitators to rethink their approach to meaningfully embedding activities. Their solution was quite novel: the language course in question took place at an imagined campground, which prompted the instructors to 'disguise' their TPR activity as communal morning exercise in preparation for the day's activities on the campground. The result was clearly an instance of authentication, which in this particular case involved not only embodiment but also enaction, or world-making, which meant that the learners were then far more willing to participate fully in the activity. The change in attitude highlights how important it is to embed an activity in a 'real-life situation'.

What sets an activity like the aforementioned one apart from those in conventional classrooms is that the entire setting centres around one common, coherent and topical theme. The activities are not separated into disconnected units, but instead are linked together and to the overall situation as a whole. For example, students in a regular second language course might be taught how to give and ask for directions in the foreign language followed by an exercise in which they imagine they are lost in an unfamiliar city. After successful completion of that exercise, which most frequently would not even require the students to leave their seats, the teacher might conceivably move on to a listening or writing exercise that has little or no connection to the previous activity. Learners in an SLE course, on the other hand, remain in one and the same environment, which has more often than not been physically recreated to replicate the target setting, and continue to use the language in related scaffolded and communicative activities.

According to the following quote, some learners might be less likely to participate fully in activities that are perceived as having no connection to the previous activity or to the learning situation as a whole:

> In a number of instances, some learners seemed to be lacking motivation, because they did not understand the current activity. In fact, their lack of motivation was even visible in their faces. Their smiles disappeared and they looked at the ceiling, yawned, and pulled out their phones. (Buring, p. 59)

This observation was also reinforced in the post-course survey: two thirds of the respondents described situations involving interactions (dialogues, scenes, games, etc.) as having a purpose and being relevant to their personal needs.

An example of relevance, or more precisely relevant vocabulary, is associated with situational and cultural sensitivity: while most SLE courses emphasise 'everyday' language, such as hobbies & interests, food, the family, etc., one team of facilitators realised that they would have to actively avoid most of these topics:

> Many of the teachers indicated that some exercises in conventional textbooks are not appropriate for teaching refugees. They specifically focus on 'sensitive' topics such as the learner's last vacation or texts discussing the family. (Scheu, p. 60)

In this course, the focus needed to be placed on a different (enacted) world in addition to learning the particular language required by the refugees.

In the SLE courses at the FTSK, the facilitators do not only emphasise movement but also the use of multiple senses wherever feasible. One very popular activity, called the labyrinth, which has frequently been used in these courses, temporarily deprives the learners of their sense of sight. The goal is to sensitize the learners to the importance of using their other senses as well to enhance learning. The labyrinth activity involves pairs of learners (one partner being blindfolded and the other not) attempting to navigate a maze that has been specifically set up by the facilitators in the classroom[21] in order to find or perhaps collect certain objects hidden within it. Because their sense of sight is no longer available to them, the learners must rely on other senses. Their means of orientation are the verbal instructions and feedback provided by their partner and the affordances they encounter as they move through the labyrinth. In this activity, which activates senses other than sight, the learners

---

21 Classroom furniture such as chairs, tables, or waste paper baskets can serve as obstacles (and provide material affordances) when designing a labyrinth.

have to express and understand instructions regarding directions, and will also have to express and understand comprehensible utterances.

As the blindfolded partners will have to partly feel their way through the labyrinth while listening to and reacting to their partners instructions (i.e. "walk forward", "slow down", "turn to the left" or "climb over the chair"), new connections can be made in the mind between hearing or feeling an object and the respective denotation. It is often feasible to include odorous and edible items (such as scented candles, soaps, foods, spices, etc.) in the labyrinth to activate other senses as well. In addition to focusing strongly on embodiment, this activity contributes to building trust between the participants (as the 'sighted' learners naturally take responsibility for their partner), therefore potentially improving group dynamics and the learning atmosphere.

Contrary to many traditional classroom activities, the labyrinth is typical of SLE activities in that it can be navigated by all students at the same time. The benefit of this is that no student feels singled out or 'put on the spot', and that every single student's time spent physically participating in the activity is maximised. In addition, there is no time wasted having most of the students watching passively as one or two students move around. Another advantage of such an activity for the learners is that, by navigating the labyrinth collaboratively but without the interference of a teacher, both their sense of autonomy and of interdependence can be enhanced. The labyrinth activity has been implemented in most SLE courses held at the FTSK so far, and the theses I have looked at do not include any reports of learners expressing a dislike for the activity. Instead, one learner specifically mentioned how much she enjoyed it:

> [I] loved the labyrinth activity! Everyone was involved in the game. [...] It was a perfect balance between fun and learning effect. (Ariane, in Buring, p. 53)

Another activity that has both a clear purpose and a real-life connection is the 'phone number' activity. After learning the numbers from one to a hundred, the students use the numbers in a situation that most people regularly encounter in their daily lives: giving someone their phone number or writing down someone else's number. Instead of simply showing their partners the phone numbers they had written down, the learners call each other up to check whether they have correctly understood one another. Not only can the learners communicate in a less exposed situation, they can also self-monitor their progress and identify their personal weaknesses with respect to the task or skill at hand. This detail was explicitly mentioned in one of the learner interviews:

> In case I had told someone the wrong number or written down somebody else's number incorrectly, the call simply did not go through. (Kerstin, in Buring, p. 46)

The Dutch course that transformed the classroom into a campsite regularly used relevant and situated activities revolving around a camping holiday. One of these was the 'backpack activity' in which students, upon arriving at the campsite and putting up their tent, were asked by the facilitators (in the role of camp counsellors) to unpack their backpacks as part of the process of settling in at camp. In this classroom, the tent consisted of four tables covered by a sheet. As the facilitators did not have access to a real tent, they improvised an alternative, reminiscent of the blanket forts that children like to build. The advantage here is that most learners will have created some facsimile of a dwelling from unconventional objects at some point in their life, and therefore can quickly adapt to the new situation and participate in the development of their learning environment. Inside the backpacks would be numerous real objects that one would expect to take on a camping holiday (for example, deodorant, toilet paper, a change of clothes, etc.) – and that the learners can be asked to bring with them from home.

While the learners unpacked their backpacks, the facilitators named the objects, and in some cases included further descriptive vocabulary such as colour or size, while the learners were able to simultaneously see, touch, and in some cases, even smell the various items. The students experienced a real-life connection between the unknown vocabulary and the objects in front of them, which enabled them to passively learn the words extremely quickly. After a few iterations, most of the learners were able to identify the objects correctly, and sort them according to various criteria (from smallest to largest, grouped by colours, objects used for personal hygiene etc.). One of the students explicitly stated how much he had enjoyed this activity and contrasted it with previous learning situations:

> When I'm sitting in [a traditional classroom], learning a language [the traditional] way always feels as if it's dead, not used in real life, like [learning] Latin. (Thomas, in Destreel, p. 32).

Activities in SLE courses differ from traditional exercises in conventional foreign language classrooms in so far as they almost always emphasise individual and relevant needs as opposed to a uniform prescribed set of skills. As outlined at some length in the first half of this book, a key assumption underlying the SLE approach is that the emergence of language can occur when relevant communication is effectively situated in authenticated activities and the learners are seen (and see themselves) as partners in the world-making process. Embodiment and sensory involvement through the use of affordances are also featured to promote scaffolded capabilities for learners to understand and express themselves, but must nonetheless be situated in a suitably authentic context, defined by its appropriate use of language, realia and the learning environment. Finally, as the various examples outlined above show, if learners are provided with a sufficient amount of varied iterations and opportunities to apply their knowledge, this can contribute to an increase in their self-confidence and help them assume responsibility for their own learning.

Chapter 8: Teaching-centred vs autonomous learning

This chapter discusses different attitudes towards autonomous learning and provides examples of how the SLE facilitators at the FTSK attempt to reconcile the principles of SLE with the deep-seated attachment that some students seem to have for traditional teaching-centred learning.

Despite receiving prior introductions to the SLE approach, a number of the learners in the SLE courses offered at the FTSK have expressed a desire for more traditional, teacher-centred lessons including, for example, overt grammar instruction:

> Since we are adults, not children, it would be useful to get some systematic grammar explanations. (Alexander, in Buring, p. 81),

and

> I would have preferred it if we had written down some grammar rules. (Astrid, ibid.)

However, as questions about grammar or grammar rules are not specifically discussed during regular class time, this type of learner might instead benefit from autonomously taking responsibility for learning grammar rules autonomously. This can be achieved in a number of ways: some students in the courses reported that they had opted to study on their own at home either using resources provided by the facilitators (predominantly tailored material focusing on the individually identified weaknesses) or availing themselves of the enormous amount of learning material available online (such as online grammar and syntax exercises, vocabulary training programs or listening comprehension activities). Depending on the initial language level, however, identifying the appropriate resource can pose a challenge for some learners, which could ultimately lead to frustration and therefore to a decline in motivation. The facilitators of at least one course set up a common online document in which learners posted their grammar questions after class for the facilitators, or other learners, to answer. This collaborative approach underlines the nature of the course: the participants help each other, fostering both team spirit and pride. Furthermore, a semi-anonymous online tool has the potential to provide even the least confident learners, i.e. those who are either too shy or not confident enough in their linguistic abilities to formulate a question in a foreign language, with a forum to voice their problems. The other option that can be employed in the courses is the post-class supplementary session.

At the FTSK, the supplementary sessions at the end of the day are held in the learners' and facilitators' native or common language, and are intended to provide both parties with an opportunity to discuss the following aspects: grammar, course content and methodology as well as personal perceptions regarding features of the course (for example, frustration, enthusiasm, bewilderment, etc.).

Due to the lack of traditional input, and often a very tight schedule, some learners are occasionally faced with uncertainties regarding language items (including grammatical or syntactical structure) throughout the day. A number of the participants were very grateful for the supplementary after-class sessions, as they provided them with an opportunity to collaboratively review the language used that day:

> There just wasn't enough time to ask questions between the various activities. And I was too embarrassed to hold up the class by asking about things from the sessions before. (Thomas, in Heinrichsohn, p. 32, my translation)

During the language discussions, learners can ask detailed questions about anything they feel they have not understood correctly. A further purpose of the supplementary sessions is to reflect on the day's activities. Learners can provide the facilitators (who, in the case of the FTSK courses, are almost all novices), with useful feedback on the activities, content and teaching techniques used, and they can also offer suggestions for improvement. The fact that the facilitators must be open to ideas and/or constructive criticism can also be considered a confirmation of the egalitarian relationship that exists between learners and facilitators. Moreover, it highlights that the courses at the FTSK are not rigidly conducted according to immutable lesson plans but rather are co-constructed by the learners and the facilitators alike. Finally, the feedback sessions can also be used to reflect on personal attitudes and feelings generated throughout the day, providing the learners with an opportunity to vent frustrations, highlight achievements or work on issues related to self-confidence.

As many courses bring together learners with varying levels of competence – learners may have previous knowledge of the language or of a related language – a potential issue is that some learners may struggle with the material, potentially causing them to feel overwhelmed. This condition is presumably not conducive to successful learning. In the post-course interview, one participant mentioned that he had trouble keeping up with the others in the group, which seems to have led to an increasing unwillingness to even ask questions during class. He noted somewhat dejectedly:

> At some point, it's just not worth asking any more questions because you won't remember the answer anyway (Mark, ibid., my translation).

In the post-class supplementary session, however, the same learner openly addressed his feelings of frustration (evidence of the importance of affect). This could be considered a sign that, while he may have been unhappy with his own progress, he had nonetheless taken responsibility for his learning. Thanks to the collaborative environment created by both learners and facilitators, the ambience created by the group was apparently so accommodating that the learner also felt comfortable enough to address his feelings. He soon realised that he was not alone in his distress and also that simply voicing the issue and receiving encouragement from all sides was enough to put him at ease: "The participant's frustration quickly dissipated during the positive feedback round" (Heinrichsohn, ibid., my translation). By situating his problem in the social (classroom) environment, the student was presumably also able to further his own development as an autonomous learner.

Two further points must be noted in this respect:
- The facilitators frequently include activities in their lesson plans for learners of varying abilities to counteract the potentially deleterious effects of boredom or frustration but cannot anticipate every potential issue.
- When learners start assuming responsibility for their learning, they can be expected to communicate their issues to the facilitator and participate in the problem-solving process.

While it might logistically be difficult to schedule a supplementary session after every single class (depending on the number of individual course sessions), the facilitators at the FTSK attempt to incorporate them as often as needed, as the evidence of their efficacy, based on the learners' feedback, has been overwhelmingly positive and visible in the learners' language and personal development (see, in particular, Heinrichsohn and Rizzo). There is no prescribed form for a supplementary session. At the FTSK, the duration and the topics discussed depend on the participants' individual needs and level of motivation. There is also no specified set of fixed questions that facilitators should ask or one way to meaningfully engage the learners. Instead, the facilitators of the SLE courses allow learners to initiate communication, as they will likely have no way of knowing what issues are relevant to the particular session or learner. The majority of the supplementary sessions at the FTSK have been more like informal gatherings and have only taken place upon request or if the facilitators believed that there might be some underlying need that the learners were not yet able or willing to communicate.

It is important to note that there is a possibility that not all students will initially adapt to a non-teacher-centred learning environment or be prepared to take responsibility for their own learning, and that this is not automatically the facilitators' fault. A few of the students in the surveyed courses were quite critical of the approach, the lack of traditional instruction, and their learning progress:

> I am not a fan of this method because we didn't write anything down. We couldn't practise the language ourselves at home. You just forget a lot. (Karin, in Destreel, p. 60),

and

> Very unusual and I definitely had to get used to it. It's alright. Not my cup of tea but I reckon it works for other people. I cannot pick up words that easily, just from having heard them one time. I need to revise them, I need to see them on a piece of paper and know their meaning. Otherwise I'm lost. (Theresa, ibid.),

or

> Most of the students argued that listening alone was not an effective method to memorise vocabulary and that writing down new words and grammar rules would have been more beneficial. (Rizzo, p. 42)

While a handful of highly critical students is to be expected in every course (see above), two additional factors may also be responsible for their opinions:
- The learners presumably did not consider that they may have been conditioned to believe that it is impossible to learn effectively outside of traditional, teacher- and notepad-centred learning environments. This might render them unwilling to truly engage in an alternative method and could therefore negate a successful learning outcome.
- Neither the approach nor the facilitators are responsible for the students' learning. Learning in the FTSK courses was successful when it was approached as a joint effort, with the main onus being on the students themselves.

Fortunately, fewer than 10% of the students maintained this initially critical opinion through the end of the course, and they were incidentally also among the students with the lowest scores in the various final assessments.

Learners who know that must see and use the written form to learn the language can broach this topic with the facilitators and request material and suggestions, or take advantage of the abundance of material available online. The fact that not all learners utilise this opportunity might also be caused by aforementioned conditioning, so it could be beneficial if facilitators emphasise the flexibility of the approach and their positive stance on suggestions and/or criticism to prevent potential prejudice as far as possible. Thankfully, some students in the FTSK courses recognised this issue, albeit after the course had already ended: "Next time, I might do myself a favour and look up words at home as well" (Lisa, in Buring, p. 81).

A further consequence of conditioning due to teacher-centred learning environments might be that not all learners will always be as responsive as one might hope. The facilitators of one course mentioned how trying the students' attitudes could be at times:

> The most challenging aspect was the passive attitude of the learners, which resulted in us [the facilitators] assuming the role of teachers again. (Rizzo, p. 36)

There are numerous reasons why learners might take a passive role in the classroom: they could be bored or tired; they could be so conditioned by their past experiences in learning situations that they simply expect to be spoon-fed by the instructor; there might be "a difference in mentality between the facilitators and the learners in regard to their relationship and roles" (ibid.); they might be sceptical of the approach and therefore not always willing to fully immerse themselves in the new environment. Some of the learners who participated in the various SLE courses were unsure whether such a radically different approach could actually work and whether they would enjoy it. Years of traditional teacher-centred learning in institutionalised education environments are bound to have a certain impact, no matter how open and flexible the learners are. However, the fact that they, and in particular those who participated without seeking credit, chose to participate in the course – despite their less than optimistic views on the likelihood of success – can be interpreted as an openness and willingness to try out something completely new. The student researcher in one of the courses surveyed her group prior to the course. She found that "more than 50% were sceptical about whether the approach would actually work" (Buring, p. 80). Nonetheless, all of the participants stated in the post-course interview that they would be interested in attending another course based on the same approach (ibid.). One of the learners even commented on overcoming her initial spontaneous reaction:

> I lost my fear. I took the first hurdle and developed a feel for the language. This approach allowed me to dabble in the language as well as the culture. (Nasri, ibid.)

Another student initially did not believe she would learn very much in such a short time but when interviewed after the course said: "I never thought I could learn so much about a foreign language in just six days!" (Katrin, in Buring, p. 78).

Similar to interaction and communication in natural or everyday settings, it is probably impossible to prepare a fixed lesson plan to deal with every eventuality. Following a rigid syllabus, with completely predefined sets of rules and activities will presumably not work in a successful SLE environment. (See the Accept Complexity beacon) The facilitator has no way of knowing how motivated the students will be that day, how long they will want to spend on each particular activity, or in what ways and with what consequences the group may decide to amend the agenda for the class, day or week.

When students are given the opportunity to voice their opinion about the learning activities and content in courses they attend, they might also begin to take responsibility for their own learning and thus become autonomous learners. The consequence, however, is that activities cannot be planned thoroughly ahead of time as there is the chance that independent learners will formulate their thoughts and request changes if they are not totally satisfied with the experience[22]. Therefore, facilitators must be aware that preparing a scaffolded and emergent learning situation may well require much more creativity, time, and effort than preparing a strictly teacher-centred lesson. For the FTSK facilitators, this meant:

- accepting and being able to deal with the fact that students may not enjoy the prepared activities,
- always having a back-up plan, and
- being able to adapt to the needs of the learners as they develop with each new situation.

As the examples have shown, moving from teacher-centred learning to autonomous learning is not always an easy undertaking. Based on the observations made in the theses, it is clear that adapting to change – especially when it affects something as fundamental as learning – required the learners and facilitators to have an open mind, the ability to reflect on their own ingrained beliefs and a willingness to explore a hitherto unknown path. Years, and in some cases decades, of learning in traditional classroom environments, in which learners are provided with input and often have little or no voice in regard to their own development, may well be the reason why some of the learners were initially sceptical of the approach. In the case of the courses referenced here, whether learners were able to overcome these deep-rooted tenets was a question of individual predisposition. However, it was nonetheless influenced by the facilitator, the learning environment and the choice of activities. By providing learners with alcoves that are reminiscent of their previous experiences in language learning, such as the post-class feedback sessions, the facilitators can attempt to assist them in their transition to becoming autonomous learners.

---

22 The more effort the facilitator has put into creating a relaxed learning environment and helping the students become successful autonomous learners, the more likely it has been that the students challenged various aspects of instruction, including the structure of the activities themselves, resulting in additional preparation work

Chapter 9: Autonomy and collaboration in the SLE classroom

This chapter takes a closer look at the roles and responsibilities of the learners and facilitators in SLE classes. Examples provided from classes held at the FTSK will highlight the importance of having participants assume responsibility for their own learning.

Learner responsibilities

Due to the types of activities and techniques geared towards language emergence, a crucial factor for the success of language courses taught according to the SLE approach is that the learners assume responsibility for their own learning:

> It was probably the strong desire to learn that I felt in this class that never made me feel as though I 'had to do something' or 'had to study' for it to please someone else. (Anne, in Nagi, p. 108, my translation)

The above quote illustrates that the learner in question seems to have been motivated by the course itself and as a result was able to disassociate learning from the common trope of 'learning as a chore'. In the courses examined in this chapter, this transformation from receptive to autonomous learner took many different forms. Some students identified a perceived lack of grammatical or syntactical knowledge in the target language and decided to remedy this weakness themselves by seeking out additional resources at home and completing grammar exercises, or simply by directly asking the facilitators for clarification in class or during the supplementary after-class sessions. The fact that the other students were able to benefit from these questions and the facilitator's answers highlights the collaborative learning effect of these interactions:

> Learners who constantly ask questions (for example, asking for the definition of new words) are involved and interested in expanding their own knowledge and, at the same time, that of their classmates. Through their

questions, they are not simply learning for themselves but they are also indirectly teaching their peers. (Rizzo, p. 39)

Other students, who felt that they needed more practice honing their writing skills, approached the facilitators and asked them for other types of assistance in, for example, finding native speaker pen pals. Finally, numerous students utilised the media resources made available by the facilitators in in-class libraries to either improve their passive language skills, learn more about the country's (popular) culture or to simply immerse themselves in the language outside of the classroom environment. Included in the majority of the emergent language classrooms at the FTSK so far, an in-class library is an area in the classroom where the facilitators place books, CDs, DVDs, and games in the target language for the learners to borrow or use during breaks. One student borrowed music CDs to take home in order to have additional exposure to the language: "I got the music from our teacher, and I listen to it every morning and at night just so I can hear the language whenever possible." (Michael, in Buring, p. 75).

There are multiple factors involved in determining whether participants are willing to take responsibility for their own learning. Unfortunately, the theses do not indicate precisely why the students developed a strong desire to learn in our SLE classes. However, the case studies analysed for this chapter provide a myriad of reasons that may well have contributed to the desired shift toward autonomous learning:

- the learning environment/classroom
- immersion in the target language and, to a certain degree, culture
- personal motivation (this includes intrinsic motivation such as wanting to communicate with a distant family member who speaks the target language, planning a holiday in the respective country or enjoying the challenge of learning a new language as well as extrinsic motivation such as finishing off a final course in a module, diversifying the degree program or improving career prospects)
- a sense of achievement (often triggered by taking successful steps towards the desirable learning outcomes)

One area where evidence of responsible learning can be found is in the students' ability to monitor themselves. According to the reports, when they themselves are able to detect progress in their own learning, they develop a sense of achievement and an inherent desire to continue along their respective learning trajectory. This can also be enhanced if their self-assessment is confirmed by the facilitator, for example in the form of encouragement:

> I am proud to see how I make progress from day to day. Today, I was able to follow the commands correctly, without having to look at someone else presenting it. The subsequent praise further increased my motivation. I also had the impression that things happened much more automatically today. (Marie, in Buring, p. 40/41)

However, self-monitoring can unfortunately also have the opposite effect (which does not negate the assumption of responsibility!):

> I feel stupid because I can't remember it and we just talked about it. [...] Everybody knows how to do it. [...] Why can't I do this?" (Johanna, in Buring, p. 41)

In this instance, the learner may have experienced frustration at her own learning pace, particularly in comparison with the other students, but she managed to remedy the situation, and as a result, was also able to overcome these feelings (see ibid.), realising that errors are not synonymous with failure. The facilitators in the FTSK attempted to assuage feelings of frustration by providing feedback, being available for discussion or praising and encouraging the learners where appropriate.

Critical readers may argue that the learners discussed in this chapter are not representative of learners in general as they are all students currently enrolled in academic degree programmes – and hence can be expected to be accomplished and motivated language learners. While this might help explain why these students on the whole have had such success with this approach, all learners are presumably capable of taking responsibility for their own learning. The three courses run by the FTSK for the *Technisches Hilfswerk* (THW), the German Federal Agency for Technical Relief, provide examples that support this argument. The participants, all active THW volunteers, sacrificed their free time to attend the courses taught by the FTSK facilitators. In addition to their day jobs, and their volunteering work at the THW, they also chose to attend one or more weekend courses to improve their English language skills. This degree of dedication was also reflected in their attitude towards learning in the course – the respective thesis does not include one single reference to uncooperative or unmotivated learners among the THW participants.

Facilitating learning: a new role for the 'teacher'

The majority of the FTSK student-facilitators had never experienced either the setting or the approach themselves. Or, as one of the THW facilitators put it, it was: "a teaching situation [...] utterly different from what [the student-facilitators] had ever experienced." (Wittner, p. 81).

Before presenting examples of the advantages and difficulties associated with the approach, the problems the facilitators faced and the successes they experienced, I would like to briefly address the special situation of one group of teachers[23] that made them stand out from the rest of the SLE facilitators: those who were involved with the *Cross Borders Project* at the FTSK. In light of the recent large-scale influx of refugees to Germany, the instructors, all students enrolled in a translator education programme with little or no teaching experience, have offered their services as volunteer teachers in a set of German courses for refugees[24]. The courses cannot truly be considered SLE courses due to the wide range of abilities and academic backgrounds of the learners, the fluctuating teaching staff and erratic attendance on the part of the learners, which ranged anywhere from no participants to up to 23 learners on a given afternoon. (Scheu, p. 15)]. However, many of the teachers nonetheless tried to incorporate SLE components into their teaching, which is why I decided to include examples from these courses in this section of the book.

To get back to the facilitators: one of the major advantages for them in the context of the FTSK courses is that they are given an opportunity to develop or hone their facilitating abilities in a relatively risk-free environment. For example, these facilitators always work in teams of at least two people (more student-facilitators were required for the THW course and the refugee course due to time constraints, the number of participants and the varying levels of Eng-

---

[23] They are referred to as teachers here because while many of them did attend an introductory workshop on the SLE approach, they did not benefit from the usual scaffolding that Don provides SLE teachers. In addition, Cross Borders is an extra-curricular initiative run by students at the FTSK and they were under no obligation to use one particular approach or another in designing and running their classes.

[24] http://crossborders-ger.blogspot.de/. During the teaching period on which the thesis referred to here is based, approximately 28 instructors taught between eight and 23 learners, four days a week for 90 minutes. There were three different language levels (literacy, beginner, advanced), which often all had to be taught on the same day and in the same group. The participants were extremely heterogeneous in terms of nationality (learners were predominantly from Syria, Afghanistan, Eritrea, Iraq and Somalia) as well as education level (some learners had no education beyond the 8th grade, while others had a BA degree). (Scheu, p. 17-19)

lish or German respectively). The team-teaching approach has proved be extremely beneficial, particularly for novice teachers, as it enables them to share experiences, and encourage and help one another during course preparation:

> I observed the different tutors and reflected on my own techniques as well. It gave me a different perspective and I came up with new techniques. (Tina, in Wittner, p. 30)

Furthermore, a second (or additional facilitator) can provide support in the actual sessions. This final point was also one of the main causes for concern that numerous student-facilitators expressed prior to their first lessons:

> [T]hey were concerned [...] that they might even black out with stage fright and not be able to teach at all. It was their primary concern that their nervousness and lack of self-confidence would cause them to fail. [...] Nevertheless, [they said] that the fact of being in a team of teachers made them more confident that everything would turn out fine." (Wittner, p. 25)

In the *Cross Borders* course, in which the levels of German and even literacy differ so greatly, working with more than one facilitator also has the added benefit of being able to split the learners into smaller groups in order to provide students at different skill levels with the appropriate language and activities. In particular, when two native speakers are present in the classroom, they engage in genuine dialogues in the Ln, thus providing learners with a wealth of natural language use to work with.

During the preparation stage, facilitators must have enough time to grow together as a team in order to develop complete trust in each other by the time the actual lessons start. If the team does not function well, or cannot hide the fact that there are tensions among them, it is likely that the learners will sense it and this may diminish the positive atmosphere of the learning environment:

> [D]uring the first two scenarios I was really nervous because I did not know what the plan was and everyone said something different. This caused confusion and chaos – nerve wracking! (Markus, in Wittner, p. 26)

A further advantage for the FTSK student facilitators is that they receive prior scaffolding for their own facilitating work from Don (and sometimes also help from other experienced facilitators). In these preparatory training sessions, the future facilitators are initially provided with an introduction to the facilitating approach(es). Don then opens the Pandora's box of relevant issues such as team work, time management, empathy, feedback and correction. Finally, Don and the participants review various tested facilitating activities and techniques before they begin to plan their lessons. This is almost always done on the basis of a sample class that Don runs in a language the participants are relatively unfamiliar with so that they can experience abductive learning for themselves (Kiraly 2015: 156). However, during these training sessions, Don is always adamant about the fact that the student facilitators should regard his contributions as guidelines or recommendations, stressing the fact that they need to discover and develop an awareness of their own personal pedagogical epistemologies in order to determine whether they can become successful facilitators:

> [Don] does not provide students with strict guidelines or a specific method to follow. Instead, students are given a great deal of freedom to interpret and integrate the principles of [the various] approaches so that they can ultimately develop their own teaching method. (Rizzo, p. 16)[25]

This preparatory step is particularly important for student-facilitators with no prior experience, or those who do not yet believe that the approach can actually work. In one case, the two would-be facilitators hired to teach one language course, both of whom had a fair amount of conventional teaching experience behind them, chose not to accept Don's offer of a series of training sessions, and instead initially implemented traditional methods and exercises. This resulted in numerous interventions by Don once the course began to shift away from the intended direction of an SLE course. This shows just how important adequate preparation can be:

> While it is only in rare instances that the advisor should intervene, he [Don] was forced to do so several times, especially during the first two days of the course. When we compared the first hours of the course to

---

25 A further result of this is that every course becomes unique and is designed for a specific group of learners.

those on the following days, the differences were striking. Whenever the students were engaged in what we might call 'traditional tasks' (in this case lecture-like presentations with a focus on the teacher), their motivation was visibly lower (they looked bored, put their heads down on the tables, etc.). By contrast, when they were engaged in more 'authentic communicative activities', they seemed far more immersed (i.e. they moved around, smiled and produced language on their own). (Buring, p. 85)

The first group of teachers in the *Cross Borders Programme* was also provided with a workshop on various teaching approaches, with a strong emphasis on SLE. However, due to the fluctuating teaching staff[26], many of the newer teachers do not have the opportunity to participate in such a workshop and have to either learn from the more experienced instructors or simply devise their own approach and teaching techniques. This naturally leads to considerable variation in the teachers' respective pedagogical approaches, which is not considered advantageous by most. In fact, in her study on the course, one student researcher found out that every single instructor would have preferred to have more information on teaching methods in order to provide the learners with a more homogenous experience (see Scheu, p. 49).

The Department of English at the FTSK offers students the opportunity to enrol in a foreign language teaching module as part of their degree program. One component of this module is a teaching internship, and most of the student facilitators discussed in this book taught their courses as a component of this module[27]. The fact that these initial teaching endeavours are incorporated into the university curriculum also means that they are provided with scaffolded assistance to develop their understanding of the approach and their facilitating skills. Hence, the student-facilitators are much more likely to really explore the potential value of this previously unfamiliar teaching approach.

In order for the SLE approach to be successful, the facilitators must be prepared to create a suitable and suitably authenticated environment in which language can emerge. This applies not only to the classroom and the type of

---

26 The course was taught both during the semester and in the term break, so not all volunteer teachers were available at all times. Also, once they graduate, most students tend to leave the university town and can therefore no longer participate in the project.

27 But all of our student-facilitators have been paid for their work as well. The FTSK's extra-curricular Language Centre has provided funding for the teaching staff at adjunct lecturer rates for most of the SLE courses we have offered to date.

activities, vocabulary and linguistic structures that are introduced but also to the facilitators' behaviour and their interactions with the learners. It hardly needs to be reiterated here that SLE facilitators must be empathetic, non-authoritarian, collaboratively inclined and pedagogically creative if they hope to create and maintain an atmosphere that is conducive to learning. The degree to which a facilitator appears to feel comfortable with and confident about using the SLE approach is sure to be apparent to the learners. In his account of his first day running a foreign language course, one of the student teachers noted:

> On the first day of class, I was not yet comfortable teaching. It was noticeable during the first activity. […] I was a bit uncertain whether the students would understand and have fun, whether the activity might not be too difficult. Don noticed that my attitude was rubbing off on the students, and he took me aside during a break and suggested that I try to be more energetic, warm and a bit less serious. I tried being more enthusiastic, open, and I made a few jokes. Suddenly, the students started to really enjoy the activity. (Destreel, p. 21)

The facilitator in question managed to maintain this modified interpersonal approach and keep the participants engaged and interested for the duration of the 25-hour course (and a subsequent one he co-taught a month later). This example not only stresses the need for appropriate preparation and a positive attitude but also the invaluable role of the expert mentor in helping the student-facilitators become successful and confident facilitators in an SLE classroom.

As touched upon in various other chapters of this book, the SLE approach is flexible in terms of the syllabus, the topics covered and the pedagogical techniques used. And to be successful it depends on co-construction. This means that facilitators require a great deal of flexibility to achieve their goal – they can never know whether it will actually be possible to realise the day's planned activities. For example, students might be too tired to participate in a certain game; it might be raining, making it impossible to leave the classroom for an outdoor activity; there might only be one student on one day and more than twenty the next, or, as was the case in one of the courses, the classroom might be locked when the class is supposed to begin. While a more experienced teacher might have found an alternative way to hold class that day, the novice facilitators were not spontaneous enough to devise another plan. They became flustered and simply waited for 30 minutes until somebody finally came to unlock the room. Unfortunately, this sense of frustration experienced by the facilitators was of course perceived by the students as well, who noted that the course that day had felt uncomfortable and rushed as the facilitators attempted to implement all of the activities written down in their lesson plan. An SLE lesson plan might therefore best be considered a general itinerary. It is by no means imperative to get through every single activity planned for a given day or even week, at the expense of harming the atmosphere within the group. Furthermore, an adaptable and open-ended lesson plan could potentially lead to more improvisation, which promotes the natural flow of language.

A challenge that Don is faced with at times, albeit often implicitly, is a certain degree of scepticism toward the proposed approach, which is hardly surprising given that the student-facilitators have all had extensive experience studying multiple foreign languages on the basis of conventional classes. Hence, many student-facilitators are initially wary of the method considering that it does not include rigid grammar and vocabulary exercises or a teacher-centred classroom set-up – all aspects they have come to expect in a language classroom, or any classroom for that matter, based on their many years of institutionalised learning. In one of the many post-course interviews, one of the facilitators explained her initial scepticism towards teaching on the basis of SLE principles: "[W]e all know that teaching is considered to be primarily achieved through discipline." (Anastasia, in Buring, p. 86). She further noted how difficult she found the first two days due to "an extreme clash of expectations" (ibid.). Fortunately, however, all of the initially sceptical student facilitators have adapted to the new situation very quickly – in most cases after the first lesson or two:

> I have a very good impression of this weekend and I am surprised at how my critical position changed towards this teaching approach. (Bianka, in Wittner, p. 29)

or

> I recognised the value of being flexible and of being able to change our plans spontaneously. It is incredible how quickly you can get used to this new teaching approach! (Olga, in Buring, p. 87).

As the refugee learners in the *Cross Borders* course have radically different needs in comparison to the groups of learners in the other foreign language courses covered in this chapter (with the possible exception perhaps of the THW courses), the teachers have to adapt and tailor the approach to meet these needs. It is therefore probably not fair to say that these teachers were sceptical of the approach in general, but that they felt they had to incorporate techniques associated with other teaching methods in order to help the refugee learners as best they could. For example, in SLE courses, emphasis is placed on the spoken language for the first 50 hours rather than the written form. This idea was initially borrowed from both *SGAV* methodology and the *Natural Approach*. In all three approaches, the spoken language is understood to be the foundation for the written language. When the latter is introduced too early, it is believed to interfere with the development of a naturalistic phonological system because learners tend to borrow the sounds from their native language in attempting to read the Ln. Withholding the written language at the beginning also encourages learners to use the panoply of senses they have at their disposal to decipher and remember word and expressions in the Ln.

However, many of the learners in *Cross Borders* courses need to focus on preparing for a language certificate examination (which tests all four basic communicative skills). They need to be able to read and fill out forms, and they require specialised vocabulary associated with formal, or 'bureaucratic' language more urgently than words related to hobbies and interests, for example (see Scheu, p. 16 and p. 40). The teachers in these courses indicated that they would have liked access to more teaching material, mainly textbooks (which are normally never found in an SLE environment). They believed that:

> ... textbooks help them achieve more structured lessons, provide them with a variety of drills and lively dialogues, and inspire them to teach relevant material. (Scheu, p. 48)

Cross Borders teachers are clearly influenced by their past experiences in institutionalised academic environments and tend to turn to traditional materials used in scholastic settings.

As explained in the previous chapter, participants in an SLE course will ideally transition from being simple receivers of input (or intake) into being autonomous learners. A prerequisite of autonomous learning is the assumption that students will take responsibility for their own learning. While the degree to which this actually occurs is presumably influenced by the learners' own motivation, both the learning environment and the relationship between the learners and their facilitators can have a significant impact on this condition. Therefore, an SLE facilitator can generally expect to need substantial preparation, not only in terms of associated techniques and activities but also regarding their own beliefs about the learning process and their perceptions of their role. It is to complement this self-reflection work that FTSK facilitators are provided with suggestions, guidance and examples of best practice to help them evolve into effective facilitators – if they find that this special pedagogical role suits them.

Chapter 10: Material affordances and the learning environment

The following chapter deals primarily with the various 'classrooms' in which the courses organised at the FTSK have taken place. The focal point is on the choice of a place for scaffolded learning, how it might be best arranged or set it up, and the extent to which SLE classrooms differ from conventional ones. After an introduction to general features of SLE classrooms and to better underline these various aspects, two distinct classrooms will be discussed that have been singled out for their innovative style.

General features of SLE classrooms at the FTSK

Due to the types of activities found in SLE courses, a traditional classroom in which students sit at desks either individually or in pairs and the teacher takes his or her position at the desk or near the board is not likely to be a suitable choice for a scaffolded language emergence setting. In terms of communicative proxemics, conventional classroom arrangements can create an unnatural distance between the facilitator and the learners and between the learners themselves, and implicitly bestow the role of purveyor of knowledge upon the facilitator. Potentially, they can also trigger memories of school and 'being taught', which, in turn, can result in more passive and diffident learners. A key assumption underlying the SLE approach is that language is likely to emerge best if one immerses oneself holistically (mentally, physically, socially and even emotionally) in the target culture and language either in a genuine Ln environment or a highly authenticated facsimile of one. Of absolutely primordial importance in an SLE classroom, where learners will be moving, role-playing, and interacting with affordances, facilitators and each other in myriad, mostly non-scholastic ways, will be the providing of plenty of space that, in its default state, is virtually devoid of typical classroom furnishings. In the conventional classrooms used for SLE courses at the FTSK, we have consistently removed almost all of the tables from the room (with the learners' help) right at the beginning of the course. They are put back only occasionally for select activities or when the course is over. We have almost always arranged the chairs in a large circle at the beginning of the course, ready to be moved out of the way or re-arranged on short notice as the need arises – which it regularly does. In this way, each group of facilitators and learners begins with a large empty space and designs its own learning environment dynamically as the course progresses.

The typically blank walls of the conventional classroom are gradually decorated with artefacts like texts, posters and even drawings that the learners create during the course of their learning activities. We have found this appropriation of the conventionally linear, rigid and lifeless classroom space to be an essential step towards changing both learners' and facilitators' mindsets with regard to the entire learning process.

Fostering a creative and proactive state of mind can be achieved not only through the arrangement of the room (i.e. the position of the facilitator(s) with respect to the learners) but also by the choice of room itself. A dark room, for example, could potentially reinforce fatigue and disinterest, while a room with large windows might literally brighten the learners' mood. A room with carpeting might be perceived as cosier by some and allow learners and facilitators to sit on the floor for certain activities. Furthermore, facilitators might consider encouraging learners to decorate the language learning room as this might help to reinforce the perception of the classroom as a reassuring non-scholastic environment and also provide students with a further opportunity to take responsibility for their own learning. The facilitators and participants in the FTSK courses also decorate or prepare the room to create an environment that reflects some features of the target culture, which encourages the learners to immerse themselves in the Ln while they are in that room. Some examples of situated classrooms created for courses discussed here include a campsite in Holland and a shared flat for visiting students in Rome As mentioned in the previous chapter, many of the course facilitators at the FTSK set up small library corners in their classrooms, with books, CDs and DVDs in the target language that the students can borrow. This encourages further authentic interaction with the language, and it also helps create a relaxed and comfortable environment, and even contributes to better personals relationships as learners see that the facilitators trust them with their own belongings.

In such an environment, students can take their first steps in the new language surrounded by other learners whom they trust and who are in the same linguistic boat. Such a classroom is particularly well-suited to the initial stages of language learning. Once students have a little more confidence in their communicative abilities in the Ln, the classroom setting can be changed in accordance with the group's respective needs. Moving the learning setting to a different location can enable learners to use the language in a more naturalistic environment – in lieu of being able to travel to the respective country. For example, facilitators (or class participants) often decide to prepare culinary specialties from a language where the Ln is spoken. Given that in most regular classrooms cooking is usually not possible, sessions can be held in a kitchen at the institution where classes are held (if one is available). This is something which is done regularly, and successfully, in almost all of the SLE courses taught at the FTSK. In this new environment, the learners are faced with an abundance of unfamiliar vocabulary related to food and cooking instructions that they can learn and experience physically, socially and linguistically.

This type of natural, everyday setting allows the learners to become immersed not only in the language per se, but also in the target culture. In some cases, cooking has even been used as one way to assess the students' progress in comprehending the Ln:

> By relying on their linguistic and collaborative competences, the learners were able to understand an authentic recipe, organise the work entirely in the foreign language and prepare lunch for all participants. (Rizzo, p. 42).

The majority of the students surveyed in the various courses in which meals were prepared together have enjoyed the activity. The sense of community and achievement, not to mention the delight of experiencing a potentially unknown dish, have been considered both enjoyable as well as beneficial to language learning. However, as one researcher noted in her assessment based on the post-course interviews, not every student has been totally convinced of the utility of this particular activity: "Some students considered the activity stressful and thought it took up an inordinate amount of time" (Heinrichsohn, p. 29, my translation). An activity that requires learners to move to a different location, and that generally demands more preparation due to the logistics involved (in cooking, for example), might therefore also be dependent on a more meticulous plan so as to avoid unnecessarily long lulls that could result in boredom, or perhaps worse, provide the students with too many temptations to communicate with each other in their native language. If time or space restrictions are an issue, even activities such as cooking can be simulated in a semi-realistic way. The facilitators of one of the shorter courses were confronted with precisely this problem and instead of foregoing the activity altogether, developed an alternative strategy. They prepared cards with pictures of all the ingredients required to prepare the dish as well as utensils and kitchen inventory, and simulated cooking in the classroom. The disadvantage is obviously that the activity was far less of a multi-sensory experience and was far more difficult to authenticate, but it did greatly reduce the logistical stress factors for both facilitators and learners. Multi-sensory, embodied and highly authentic activities would of course fit in far better with the SLE approach, but compromises will sometimes be necessary depending on a multitude of factors.

Food is generally a much appreciated topic for language learners at all stages, and especially beginners perhaps because most of the material, social and experiential affordances involved are very familiar to everyone. And, unless the facilitators have already purchased all the necessary ingredients prior to the activity, this gives the group a further opportunity to utilize a more natural venue in which to learn, with its attendant affordances. If it is logistically feasible to visit a supermarket, accompanying the students on a grocery shopping trip can serve as a very natural and genuine situation in which to use a new language. The learners can discuss what products need to be bought and how much they need prior to setting out. In the shop or supermarket itself, students can compare prices and quality (depending on their current abilities) and come to mutual agreements. In doing so, they not only use the newly learned vocabulary and structures but might also extrapolate entirely new information from each other, the facilitators, and their surroundings. In some cases, SLE learners at the FTSK have been able to interact with other customers, the cashier or a waiter (for example at one of several local ice cream shops, cafés or even restaurants where the Ln is spoken by the employees). This has proven to be invaluable to them in terms of gaining confidence in both their passive and active communicative skills.

Scavenger hunts are another activity that can help move the classroom from the more conventional (and pedagogical) classroom setting to a more natural communicative one. As in the case of cooking or going shopping, on a scavenger hunt students can experience Ln or words, expressions and structures associated with affordances in more natural surroundings and with all their senses. Learners who find all the clues or fulfil all the tasks specified in the activity will be filled with a heightened sense of achievement, as most scavenger hunts take place outside of the familiar classroom environment and without the supervision of the facilitator. Learners navigate 'new' surroundings and, due to the facilitator's absence, must truly take responsibility for their own learning and self-discipline in not simply resorting to their native language to accomplish their experiential goals. Alternatively, facilitators can accompany the learners on an excursion through town to learn, for example, directions and the names of the various institutions, shops and other municipal structures they might find. The linking of words to features of the world experienced directly and in a multi-sensory manner has proven to be a tremendous aid to memory for our learners.

All outdoor activities can be followed up in the classroom later on. After walking around town with their students, the facilitators of one course presented the learners with a map of the same town, allowing them to use the previously experienced vocabulary and phrases. Having just seen the buildings and walked up and down the streets, the learners could easily adapt these fresh multi-modal memories to the new, more abstract, activity, and they demonstrated great skill in navigating from one point to another on the map.

If, due to the location of the institution or weather conditions, facilitators do not have the option of taking their learners to more authentic settings outside of the classroom or building, they can always opt to (re)create particular settings in the classroom itself. As the course that 'took place' in Italy could not include a visit to Rome, the facilitators instead used paper taped to the floor to recreate a map of the city as well as pictures of the various sights. This provided the learners with the opportunity to 'navigate' the streets themselves and learn about the most important buildings and monuments. A near natural mock-up, authenticated through the use of affordances relevant to the target culture and setting, is not only an excellent environment to potentially put the students at ease and foster a common objective, it also allows facilitators to implicitly include iterations for the learners' benefit, as the following example highlights. Supermarkets, in which the facilitators (and at a later stage the learners) act as shop keepers, have been recreated inside several of the SLE language classrooms. The students can use real or play money and can attempt to 'purchase' a variety of items. In one of these scenarios, the shop keeper was an older lady with a hearing impediment. By pretending to not understand the students when they asked, for example, for the price of their desired item, she was able to repeat the target utterance numerous times and therefore implicitly correct potential mistakes. This is a good example of authentication where both the learners and the facilitators were well aware that the facilitator playing the role of the shop keeper was not really deaf. But everyone behaved as if she were and the students were able to benefit from the repetitious authenticated speech of the shop keeper. This made the entire scenario more authentic, and therefore more believable. When activities are authentic, they gain relevance for the learner and trigger a personal connection, which can lead to improved learning outcomes:

> During all activities with the whole group, when I could see a real-world connection, when I could see a personal connection – that is when I had 'aha' moments. (Nina, in Buring, p. 56)

Two examples of special SLE classrooms

A classroom setting that deserves a special mention was the one prepared for one of the Italian courses. During the first lesson, instead of explaining goals, expectations, and the approach behind the course, the facilitators greeted the learners as if they were all exchange students from around Europe who had all just arrived in Rome for a six-month Erasmus exchange. (As is the case for all SLE courses offered at the FTSK, this one was conducted completely in the Ln, Italian in this case. None of the learners had any significant knowledge of Italian beforehand). With the help of cognates, pictures, screen-shots and gestures, the facilitators made it clear that they would be helping the learners adapt to life in Rome. In this way, the facilitators not only set the stage for the entire course but also took the first steps towards creating a sense of community. The first task that needed to be accomplished was to arrange for housing for 22 students in Rome. The facilitators first got the learners to choose a shared flat they wanted to inhabit from among the offerings of an online real estate agency. Subsequent activities focused on 'furnishing' and decorating the rooms of the flat with props including homemade furniture that the facilitators had made in advance. The subsequent course activities were all derived from the 'six months in Rome' theme and included learning to use the metro system, investigating Rome in terms of commercial and institutional venues as well as visiting the touristy sights of the city, enrolling in courses at the university, seeing a doctor for the treatment of minor medical issues, going to a café and a restaurant and making an excursion by bus to Florence. The entire course was accompanied by a second theme: Italian cooking. The group actually learned how to make a range of Italian dishes over the course of the two week class, and they did all of the cooking, shopping and even cleaning up every day – and all in Italian. These two themes in fact provided the structure for the entire 50-hour course, with each activity being designed to build on the previous one.

This type of direct active involvement in the course, right from the beginning, offers numerous advantages. The learners begin to gel as a team while simultaneously discovering each other's creative sides and they also become acquainted with their first Italian words (furniture, different rooms in an apartment, buildings in a city, kitchen utensils and grocery items) and a wide variety of functional language elements.

According to the learners' own reports, the classroom transformation not only cultivated a sense of community but also helped to create an environment in which the learners could feel at ease: "We transformed the room into a flat during the course, which made it seem less like a university classroom" (ibid., p. 25, my translation), or "The setting was so similar to a real flat that it started to feel like a second home" (Karla, in Rizzo, p. 42). Before the activity, the learners had already chosen Italian names for themselves, which they agreed to use exclusively for the duration of the course.

The facilitators' choice of an imaginary but plausible learning situation, a group of Erasmus students in a shared flat, tapped into the learners' prior knowledge and ensured that, due to the learners' age and status as university students, everyone involved could relate to the entire situation. Hence, authentication posed no problem at all. Furthermore, choosing a coherent and situated setting ensures that the vocabulary learned throughout the course remains topical, relevant and appropriate for scaffolded learning (the areas of vocabulary covered many aspects of student life: home life, university, cooking, etc.).

Another exemplary natural classroom setting was created in the English courses taught on site at the *Technisches Hilfswerk* (THW), the German Federal Agency for Technical Relief. As the THW operates in global crisis and disaster areas, they must regularly train for deployments abroad. To this end, the THW has a training site, its so-called 'disaster city', to simulate operations in areas afflicted by conflict or natural disaster. The 'disaster city' proved to be an ideal environment to nurture language emergence among the THW participants as it both beautifully simulated the required communicative setting and included all or most of the necessary realia that the volunteers would use in real disaster situations.

As the theses reveal, it is not necessary to perfectly replicate the future communicative setting or use completely authentic learning materials. But visual stimuli and familiarity with the surroundings/objects can lead to improved outcomes. In this case, the opportunity to work with the participants on site was a major advantage as it provided the learners with the necessary affordances to allow them to authenticate the learning activities without problems. Facilitators and participants in the THW course were also granted access to one of the THW trucks that transport the equipment regularly needed by relief workers. In the case of the THW course, the choice of 'classroom' was of particular importance as most common language institutions do not stock the respective relevant resources or materials (fire hoses, stretchers, metal detectors, etc.).

As the participants were allowed and in fact encouraged to make use of their own resources, the relationship between learners and facilitators became even more egalitarian, as the learners were the experts in terms of assembling and handling the equipment and they could therefore 'teach' their facilitators. Even though the facilitators diligently prepared the course with the appropriate terminology, they could not be expected to be familiar with every piece of equipment used by the THW. The case study on this course even notes that "[the student-facilitators] were worried about not knowing the needed technical vocabulary" (Wittner, p. 27). By sharing responsibility with the learners, however, they were able to focus more of their attention on creating a suitable environment for natural and scaffolded language learning. Such a situation surely nurtures self-confidence, which is a prerequisite for positive learning outcomes and helps to modify the traditionally assigned role of the all-knowing teacher.

Designing an appropriate learning space does not necessarily require facilitators to spend large amounts of money or time on preparation. Creative solutions to imitate an authentic or natural environment can be extremely cost-effective by using material found in the classroom (see the labyrinth activity that uses mainly classroom furniture), bringing in props from home or asking learners to bring in own material (see the imagined campsite, shared flat, or supermarket) or creating the material together with the students. Involving the learners in the design of the room also greatly reduces the time needed to create the space and has the added benefit of encouraging co-construction.

A chapter dedicated to choosing or setting up a classroom might initially seem slightly surprising to some readers as, in many cases, teachers do not necessarily have a say in where they would like to teach. However, as the principles of SLE courses include the need to create naturalistic, authenticated communicative situations, the choice of an appropriate environment can ultimately be one of the defining factors for the success of a course. The perfect classroom template does not exist: a suitable setting for learning is contingent on the students' needs and desired outcomes. It could be confined to one room, located outdoors, or periodically move from one space to the next. The only definitive requirement is for the chosen 'classroom' to put the learners at ease, allow them to experience the target culture as much as possible, and provide sufficient opportunities for authentic and relevant language to emerge.

Chapter 11: Beyond teaching – From scaffolding to emergence

The last chapter of this section deals with Jerome Bruner's concept of scaffolding, which is related to Vygotsky's Zone of Proximal Development (ZPD) and was discussed at various points in the first half of the book. Unlike teaching or instruction, scaffolding refers to support for learner-initiated learning. It tends to be more extensive at early stages of learning, and is gradually reduced as learners' need for it declines. In addition to scaffolding, this chapter will also focus on the Ln-only imperative, proleptic error correction and documented instances of emergence.

The Ln-only imperative

The value of having foreign language classes held partly, primarily or solely in the Ln has been a matter of considerable debate for some time, and there seems to be no consensus on this point (see Macaro 2001). It is interesting to note, however, that the American Council on the Teaching of Foreign Languages recommends that at least 90% of the interaction in foreign languages take place in the Ln. (see Crouse 2012: 23). And as Macaro (2001: 532) reports, the National Curriculum for England states that the target language should be used for most communication in the foreign language classroom. The learners in the SLE courses at the FTSK courses, who, for the most part, are used to rigid adherence to the syllabi and strict rules that tend to prevail in conventional language classrooms – as they have experienced during their time spent in scholastic learning environments – are often surprised by the flexible and relaxed atmosphere that is typical of SLE courses. Learners are never forced to speak, the pace of learning varies from learner to learner, and the Ln is understood to be co-constructed by everyone in the group, working collaboratively. Perhaps the only recommendation that comes close to a 'rule' is that all communication must take place in the target language and not in the learners' native tongue(s).

Based on my interpretation of the various quotes in this section, speaking exclusively in the foreign language can cement a common, and therefore united, sense of learning. It can be perceived as putting all the students on equal footing and therefore in a position where they can help each other reach a point where understanding, and later using, the language no longer seems an inaccessible objective. The classroom has the potential to become a microcosm of the target language culture in which learners and facilitators alike become partners in constructing and communicating through joint creative efforts. Some data also suggest that, if the learners communicate with each other in their common or native language, they need a lot of time and must make a great effort to find their way back into the foreign language: "It is hard to get back into [the foreign language] after speaking German or hearing somebody speak German" (Andreas, in Buring, p. 35).

Many of the learners in the FTSK courses initially struggle with the one-language requirement. One of the authors of the theses on which this section is based noticed that even though the learners were instructed to only speak in the foreign language, they sometimes strayed back to their common language. The main reasons for these lapses were:
- students were unsure whether they had correctly understood instructions/explanations,
- they thought they could get away with it as the instructors could not hear them, or
- "they wanted to communicate but were lacking the [...] words and could not express themselves with gestures" (Buring, p. 34).

However, if the learners are able to overcome these initial hurdles, they may identify the benefits and recognise their own progress:

> The instructors were talking to us [in the foreign language]. At first I felt unhappy because I didn't understand a word. Then you just accept what is going on, you just have fun. You're happy because at some point you understand what is going on [...]. After the first, second or third day, you understand a conversation in the [foreign language]. That is amazing. (Katja, in Buring, p. 35)

When questioned about their motive for speaking in their mother tongue in the retrospective interviews, one of the participants pointedly noted: "We're used to talk[ing] in our native language. It's easy to slip back into it." (Janine, in Buring, p. 34). I believe this is a notion that many readers can sympathise with or might even have experienced themselves. When you are used to always talking to someone in one language, it can feel almost alienating to address that person in a different language. The facilitators in these courses attempt to alleviate this situation by creating an appropriate and anxiety-free environment (see the roles of the facilitators and the significance of the classroom) in which students feel comfortable enough to allow learning to take its natural course – without the desire to remain in the safe haven that is the native language. Fortunately, the facilitators in the FTSK courses receive sufficient prior (and ongoing) assistance and are, for the most part, able to avoid these situations. One of the strategies employed by FTSK facilitators is to approach learners who are speaking in their native language, and to address them in the foreign language. In many cases, the learners might not consciously realise that they are de facto 'breaking the rules', and a friendly reminder is all it takes to convince them to attempt to communicate exclusively in the foreign language again. The facilitator of one of the courses did, however, note that this method was quite challenging, as it required him to be hyper-vigilant all the time and he did not want to give the students the impression he was listening in on private conversations (see Destreel, p. 16).

Another strategy used in many of our SLE courses is to create a new identity for the students by giving them names in the foreign language. This approach can help the learners to actively focus on the target language imperative by embedding it in an authentic setting:

> Creating a new 'identity' for the learners was essential for two reasons. First, it helped create distance between the German environment outside of the classroom and the foreign language environment inside. Secondly, it encouraged students to move beyond the traditional detachment that often exists between teachers and learners towards a collaborative relationship between learners and facilitators as both peers and co-constructors of the course. (Rizzo, p. 25)

Fortunately, many of the FTSK learners recognise the importance of this issue early on and decide to take responsibility for their own learning by actively avoiding students who are not speaking in the foreign language (see Buring, p. 35). As many instances of students slipping back into their native language have taken place during breaks, and the facilitators naturally cannot be expected to follow the learners everywhere they go and police their behaviour, providing target language break options can be very useful. In one course, learners on their lunch break, for example, could watch videos in the Ln set up by one of the facilitators. This not only reinforces the Ln-only imperative but also provides the students with an opportunity to learn more about (popular) culture and to experience more of the Ln outside of the classroom. One of the students in this course mentioned how much he enjoyed this offer and even recognised the 'hidden' intention: "We could focus on the video and totally forgot to speak German." (Marek, in Destreel, p. 37).

The target-language imperative naturally also applies to the facilitators. SLE facilitators communicate exclusively in the foreign language in the classroom – no matter whether they are giving instructions or answering questions, planning the next lesson with the group or introducing new vocabulary or linguistic structures. This might initially feel slightly alienating for the students but, if an appropriate pace is adopted and the vocabulary used is tailored to the students' level of comprehension, and if there are sufficient iterations and teachers also use non-verbal communication, the learners can very frequently figure out what the facilitators were trying to communicate:

> I sometimes had trouble understanding the teachers, but it wasn't so bad because the context, their facial expressions or just certain words helped me to understand. (Anina, in Destreel, p. 60)

Learners can also rely on each other in these situations. If one learner has understood the instruction and begins to participate, the other students can follow his or her lead. However, facilitators must ensure that the learners do not simply translate what has been said into the shared language.

Scaffolding and the Importance of Affect in the SLE Classroom

The scaffolding approach in SLE courses is evident both in the classroom activities as well as in the facilitators' language. In the early phases, the facilitators generally speak at a slightly reduced speed and use shorter, very clearly enunciated sentences. This promotes comprehension, and hence also learner confidence, at a stage at which the participants have a very limited vocabulary or understanding of the grammar, and little experience with the natural sound and flow of the target language. As the course progresses, the pace picks up, sentences become longer, and the facilitators pronounce words more naturally in order to attune the learners' ears to natural language use and encourage scaffolded abduction. As there is no obligation to speak in these courses, requests and questions are also phrased in such a way as to not single out individual students. Instead of "X, would you please…?", the facilitators formulate indirect requests: "Who would like to…?". This allows students to autonomously decide if and when they are ready to actively use the new language and presumably does not induce feelings of potential anxiety. Fortunately, the FTSK facilitators were very seldom faced with learners who were simply too shy or unwilling to participate. In these extremely rare cases, however, it might be conceivable for facilitators to perform the desired task themselves, to transform the activity into a whole group activity, or to focus on non-verbal communication instead.

Empathetic facilitators might initially run the risk of over-adapting their language while communicating with the learners. It is, after all, quite an undertaking to simply ignore a student who seems visibly bewildered and to continue on at a suitable pace. The FTSK facilitators attempted to remain aware of this issue and tried to counteract it as much as possible by using their hands and bodies, modelling the action or showing pictures to convey meaning in addition to the spoken utterances. In some of the courses, the facilitators invited guests to interact with the students or present a culturally relevant topic. The advantage of having guest speakers is that they can be expected to speak at a natural speed and not adjust their language to the students' level. Also, the students will have to fine-tune themselves to the new voice, possibly a new accent or dialect, and unknown vocabulary and linguistic structures. Once the learners realise that they are able to follow the native guest speaker's presentation, they will hopefully develop a sense of pride and achievement, potentially providing them with the confidence to engage in further natural communicative situations in the future.

The culmination of this scaffolding approach is then genuine communication outside of the classroom. While the facilitators and learners of a Hungarian course managed to organise an actual week-long trip to Budapest (see Nagi), other courses that were more restricted in terms of time and logistics, decided to find natural situations in the vicinity (see Chapter 10).

Activities emphasising emergence rely on the 'understanding-expression' dichotomy and are scaffolded according to the learners' level of competence. When new words or structures are introduced, the learners are merely expected to recognise or basically understand them. One way this is tested by the student-facilitators at the FTSK is by showing pictures of the respective words and asking the learners to point to the correct image. As communicative competence emerges, the activity is then adapted repeatedly, with the facilitators providing simple descriptions, slightly more difficult descriptions, ambiguous descriptions or synonyms and antonyms. In a later stage, learners can then be asked to either name or even describe the word in question themselves. The activity, referred to by Don as the 'fly swatter activity' (as it involves using a fly swatter to tap a card taped to the blackboard bearing the word, picture or object named or described by teacher[28]), is played in two or three competing teams and has been used in every course so far as it requires very little material, can be used at virtually any stage of language learning, and promotes team spirit. It also brings out the students' competitive side, a fact that many learners mentioned favourably in their respective interviews or surveys (the activity was described by the students as "fun", "enjoyable", "challenging", "competitive", etc.). It is worth keeping in mind, however, that not all students have a competitive streak and might therefore not enjoy the activity as much as others. One student criticised the activity and justified his response by saying: "I am just not really a competitive person" (Timo, in Destreel, p. 34). In order to avoid discontent among the students, the facilitators ensure that not all activities entail an element of competition and also include sufficient activities in which the learners can grow together as a group.

As a general rule, one might say that a teacher in a traditional classroom provides basic rules to the learner prior to an activity, while the SLE facilitators at the FTSK attempt to nudge the learners towards increased communicative competence through natural communication in the form of role play, videos, games, debates and conversation.

Proleptic error correction

In scaffolded language emergence classes, the initial emphasis is exclusively on language reception, or comprehension. Students are never forced to speak in the foreign language and may independently decide when to utter their first words in the new language. The justification of this approach is that a student who is consumed by anxiety, which might be induced by forcing students to do something they are not comfortable with (especially if they believe they will make mistakes), will presumably not learn effectively. One of the student researchers found that the learners seemed more relaxed and smiled when they used language when they were ready and when the incentive to speak came from within. Conversely, they tended to come across as frustrated or even

---

[28] With younger learners, it might be a good idea to use inflatable objects in the place of fly swatters to avoid potential injury as they might be tempted to swat each other.

embarrassed when they were forced to speak, for example when asked to respond to a teacher's questions or instructions individually before the entire group (see Buring, p. 37): "One time I had to play a role in a 'restaurant scene' and I had the feeling of making a fool of myself" (Silvio, in Buring, p. 39). In the assessment of the retrospective interviews, one researcher found that this sentiment was shared by a number of learners:

> Four out of 18 [students] wrote that they felt comfortable [speaking in front of the group of learners and facilitators], the rest felt frustrated, exposed, or overwhelmed. (Buring, ibid.)

Based on my personal experience teaching both young learners and adults, the "fear of making a fool of yourself" tends to prevail more strongly in adults who are no longer as in touch with their 'playful' side. However, fear of failure is presumably also much more stressful to adults as they may often have been conditioned to being mistake-averse due to their educational or professional backgrounds. Facilitators might consider keeping these points in mind when working with adult learners so as to ensure that these types of situation do not arise or can be circumnavigated if they do.

As the learners' knowledge of the language is probably still minimal and they are not likely to previously have been immersed in the culture, facilitators expect the learners to make mistakes in the early stages of communication. In traditional language learning settings, teachers often immediately draw attention to mistakes; this is surely not because they are malicious, but because they see mistakes as an opportunity to highlight problems, involve the entire group of learners, and ultimately improve the learning process. However, these corrections can often have the opposite effect. Shy learners, for example, with little confidence in their own abilities may need numerous sessions to muster up the courage to speak in a foreign language in front of a group of de facto strangers. By publically highlighting their mistakes, facilitators could inadvertently embarrass the student or rob them of the little confidence they have. Depending on the learner and the context of the language course, this could result in the student either refraining from participating in activities (and thus reducing the learning effect) or even their withdrawal from the class[29]. A further undesirable consequence of misdirected corrections might be the creation of a depend-

---

29 This point becomes particularly pertinent when students are voluntarily enrolled in a class or not relying on a grade.

ency relationship. If students are corrected too often or in an inappropriate manner (for example, by interrupting the natural flow of speech), they could lose confidence in their communication skills and begin to rely on the teacher for correction in order to use only 'correct' language:

> I always want to be corrected. Otherwise, I will make mistakes over and over again. I want to be told immediately whether what I am saying is correct. That way, I feel more certain about the language and I am more inclined to try out new words. (Marina, in Buring, p. 81)

As it can be assumed that the majority of learners neither want nor can resort to their teachers in every natural communicative situation, developing a dependency on the facilitator obviously becomes a hindrance to language use. In light of these consequences, the facilitators in the SLE courses tend to opt for a more indirect approach to correction.

Instead of emphasising a mistake, and consequently putting the student who made the error on the spot, the facilitators in the FTSK courses offer proleptic feedback. In concrete terms, this means that only minimally invasive corrections are made, and only when the comprehensibility of the message is in danger, as fluency is given precedence over accuracy[30]. While facilitators at the FTSK do not try to anticipate potential errors, they must be constantly alert so as to identify errors that appear frequently within a group (for example during group activities in which the students are all using similar vocabulary/structures). Once identified, the facilitators attempt to nudge the learners towards the correct usage of the misused term, expression or phoneme. They mainly achieve this by recasting or reformulating sentences with the correct term, expression or phoneme. Understandably, not all facilitators are able to immediately implement this non-traditional approach to error correction. Due to their own experience in learning foreign languages, and presumably some form of initial scepticism toward the method, the facilitators of one course decided to use traditional display questions[31]. The outcome, however, was far from ideal. As the student researcher noted:

---

30 This is also the reason why pronunciation or terms/expressions are 'corrected' more frequently than syntax or grammar.

31 Display questions are used to check whether students have learned/remembered previously taught structures, words, etc. Examples of display questions include: "What is the past tense of 'to go'"?, or "How do you say this? [holds up flashcard]"

The facilitators were checking the students' grammar and pronunciation skills. This led almost half of the students to feel concerned about their pronunciation skills. (Buring, p. 64)

Learning how to give constructive and non-invasive feedback on errors is therefore an extremely important skill for a facilitator. Among the most successful and non-invasive instances of error correction in the FTSK courses have occurred when the learners are not really aware that they are being corrected. This can be achieved through peer correction, self-correction or as an integral component of an activity.

From my experience, many traditional instructors tend to focus on every single mistake, and, consequently, the student who has made the mistake which, depending on the learner, may have negative consequences for the learning outcome. A further consequence of this approach is that it can condition learners to fear mistakes:

A common point of criticism was that the facilitators could not pay attention to everyone during activities in smaller groups and therefore could not correct all mistakes. Many learners worried that they would internalise incorrect phrases (Heinrichsohn, p. 32, my translation),

It can also make them almost crave correction:

All surveyed participants agreed that they wanted to be corrected, ideally by having the facilitators repeat the sentence correctly. They felt the resolved mistake should then be stressed in the corrected sentence (ibid., own translation).

By providing only constructive feedback, the learners might ultimately come to realise that making mistakes in a natural communicative situation is not as catastrophic as they seem to believe it is: "In real dialogue activities, despite slight mispronunciations or the use of the wrong article, communication was successful." (Buring, p. 64) Unfortunately, however, a successful communicative situation is not always enough to convince learners of the merits of fluency over accuracy. As one of the participants noted: "I'd rather say something when I'm sure it's right and I [have] had enough time to think about it." (Anna, in Buring, p. 39) While she confirms that students should by no means be forced to speak, her comment also seems to highlight her ingrained fear of making mistakes. As the aims of these courses include creating within the learners themselves the basic foundations of the language upon which to scaffold further progress, developing sufficient confidence to use the language autonomously, and assuming responsibility for one's own learning, the key focus needs to be on the ability to communicate effectively – not on flawless, near-native language use. Once again, the environment within the foreign language classroom can also have a positive effect on students' attitudes to making mistakes. The more accommodating the surroundings, and the stronger the team spirit, the less likely some of the FTSK learners were to avoid communication for fear of errors: "I always felt very comfortable. I wasn't afraid to make mistakes" (Philipp, in Destreel, p. 41).

Furthermore, in a successful SLE environment, the learners will, over time, theoretically develop the necessary proficiency to correct their own mistakes, sometimes with the help of their peers, which in turn might reduce their desire for constant correction.

As previously discussed, one of the primary emergent outcomes of scaffolded language emergence courses and the SLE approach in general is the assumption of responsibility for autonomous learning on the part of the students. By assuming responsibility for their own learning and as a direct result of the scaffolded approach, autonomous learners are more likely to either implicitly or explicitly express a desire to make fewer mistakes during language use at some point in the learning process. A quote from one of the many post-course surveys illustrates this point: "The better I became at the language, the more importance I attached to making fewer mistakes." (Tina, in Nagi, p. 109, my translation). This observation illustrates two of the points made so far:

- If students assume responsibility for their own learning, they might independently set their own learning objectives, and
- Students do not necessarily require immediate correction to improve their skills – once a certain level is reached (which likely differs from learner to learner and learning objective to learning objective), an inherent desire to speak the language 'properly' can automatically emerge.

Emergence

In the introduction to this section, I mentioned that I was faced with two rather major issues in preparing this meta-case study, one of which being that it is extremely difficult to isolate the various aspects discussed in the theses due to the holistic and interwoven nature of this approach. Instances of emergence, which I consider a particularly vital aspect, were the most difficult to pinpoint and present in a dedicated section. I personally believe that the examples in these chapters, whether they are related to a change in attitude, increased self-confidence, or improved deductive language skills are, in and of themselves, all evidence of emergence. However, one of the theses consulted for this book fortunately included some specific quotes that point to possible cases of emergence.

1) An increase in non-explicitly taught vocabulary:

One day, the student researcher overheard the learners telling the facilitator that they had recognised a phonetic similarity and wanted to ask her for clarification. Based on this new information, they invented their own game to practise similar phrases. In this case, emergence had presumably joined forces with the assumption of responsibility for one's own learning and resulted in a more differentiated vocabulary. The learners also realised that something different was happening here and that their learning was progressing in a way that many of them were not used to:

> All of a sudden, I could remember a few words and could even ask for a person's name, although I had not explicitly focused on it. It was just there, out of nowhere. (Katja, in Buring, p. 70)

or

> We could apply a lot of things actively that we had acquired only passively during the first hours. (Anna, ibid.)

and

> The facilitators point to a green scarf, a green table, a green leaf. You hear it over and over again. At some point, the word 'green' just gets stuck in your head. (Miriam, ibid., p. 71)

2) A 'sudden' understanding of grammar

Even though they were never taught linguistic rules, and were provided with virtually no explanations of grammar by the facilitators (except for the occasional point that arose in the supplementary session), the students managed to infer numerous grammar rules just by listening to the facilitators and following their commands in various instances, including TPR activities. Based on her post-course survey, one researcher noted:

More than three quarters of the respondents said that, by the end of the course, they had learned many things about the grammar[32] although there had been no explicit grammar instruction. (Buring, p. 70)

This was further substantiated by one of the learners herself:

At some point, I noticed that every time I use the first person singular, the verb ends with the same suffix. I felt quite proud that I had figured the rule out by myself. (Maleika, in Buring, p. 71)

3) Independent use of the foreign language:

Successful instances of immersion and emergence have the potential to help the learners feel more comfortable in their independent use of the foreign language. After just six days of instruction, a large number of the participants in one course already felt confident enough to use the language independently. According to the post-course interview:

> [...] half of the learners stated that they felt ready to communicate in the foreign language outside of the classroom in a limited way. Six respondents said that they were comfortable speaking with friends or acquaintances (Buring, p. 75).

One student even admitted that "she accidentally spoke to her flat mates in the foreign language one morning." (ibid.)

---

32 For example, they had learned to differentiate between 1st, 2nd and 3rd person singular and 1st person plural – forms typically used in group TPR activities.

Conclusion

When learners first encounter scaffolded and emergent language courses, they often find themselves faced with a number of previously unfamiliar techniques, activities, and a learning approach that is based on affordances and autonomous learning as opposed to rules and input. They are required to assume responsibility for their own learning and to participate in the co-construction of not only the classroom environment but also the course itself. Instead of sitting at their desks and being spoon-fed new vocabulary and/or grammatical structures, they experience the language with their body and all of their senses. Their mistakes are not overtly corrected; instead the facilitators provide only proleptic feedback on errors. They are confronted with (and asked to use) the foreign language from the moment they set foot in the classroom, as the facilitators communicate exclusively in the target language – whether they are giving instructions or introducing new language items. And they are never required to speak until they decide they are ready to do so. In order to encourage this process, the facilitators scaffold their language to the learners' levels, thereby promoting self-confidence and autonomy and, ultimately, enabling natural and authentic communication to emerge.

The purpose of this section has been to give readers some examples of how the principles of *Second Language Emergence* courses have been applied, and are still applied, at the FTSK. My intention was not to provide templates for activities or classroom design, but instead to showcase their reported advantages or disadvantages as well as the numerous different ways in which they were perceived by the learners. The authentic examples that focus on the facilitators and learners are naturally unique and provide only a glimpse of the various (pre)dispositions and attitudes that might exist in an SLE environment. Nonetheless, I hope that these practical examples adequately exemplify the theoretical aspects discussed in the first section.

Don Kiraly

SECTION III: A PROLOGUE... INSTEAD OF A CONCLUSION

Chapter 12: Initial guidelines for Scaffolded Language Emergence facilitators

This brief chapter comes at the end of this introductory volume on SLE but it is far more a prologue than a conclusion. Its function is to offer would-be scaffolded language emergence facilitators some initial guidance for creating and implementing their own SLE courses. Having worked with many teams of novice SLE facilitators over the course of the past ten years, I have tried to nudge and foster the incipient emergence of their SLE course design and facilitating skills, but without purporting to suggest that there are rules of any sort that they must follow. SLE is, after all, an approach and not a method. I see it as a range of emergent paths that SLE facilitators – including me – will continue to shape by walking them. The following guidelines should hence be understood in terms of advice based on my personal experience rather than as authoritative instructions – even though I must admit that the conviction with which they are expressed may suggest the latter. I have placed particular emphasis on points that I have found essential for my own facilitating work and that have proven to be helpful for would-be facilitators in the process of designing and running their own SLE courses, but each facilitator will naturally have to consider the value and utility of these recommendations from their respective individual perspective.

Creating an emergent learning environment: a focus on affordances and a role for instruction

As should be very clear to our readers at this point, I believe that teachers can begin to evolve into facilitators by adopting a perspective that sees language learning more as an emergent phenomenon within each individual and group of learners than as a process of ingestion or accumulation of linguistic structures or language rules. Rather than trying to 'teach' a language to learners or provide some hypothesised innate language acquisition device with 'input', the assumption underlying the SLE approach is that facilitators should instead take advantage of material, social and experiential affordances to encourage learners to communicate with the extra-linguistic tools at their disposal – gradually expanded to include the new foreign language – while leaving their native language and other languages they might know outside the classroom. (Those languages are of course still in the learners' minds and can hardly be turned off completely, but tackled with effort and concentration, engaged exposure to the new Ln combined with body language can work together to allow the new language to emerge).

In order to provide a coherent communicative environment that learners will be willing and able to authenticate readily, I recommend that facilitators organize their SLE courses in a tripartite hierarchical manner, starting with a general overarching theme for a two- or three-week course, and then subdividing that main theme into a set of sub-themes (perhaps one per class day), and finally, within the scope of the sub-theme for the day, implementing a series of concrete in-class learning activities (each of which might last for up to an hour each). The overall theme for a course might, for example, be a culinary odyssey in the target culture, an imaginary trip to a city where the Ln is spoken, or even an educational tour to different parts of the foreign country. The structure of the course would devolve logically and coherently from the chosen basic theme. The facilitators might choose the set of interrelated sub-themes themselves, but they might also decide to seek the complicity and collaboration of the learners in the process of syllabus design. A "trip to a foreign country" theme might yield sub-themes including, for example: preparing items to take on the trip, making hotel arrangements, traveling to the foreign country by plane, settling in at the destination, and exploring the new environment. Concrete activities that could be used to address the sub-themes in classwork might involve: selecting clothes and other personal items for the trip (including learning the names of items of clothing as well as items for personal hygiene and other objects one might take on trip), learning adjectives that one might need to specify the desired features of lodgings, learning the numbers from one to 100 in order to be able to identify room numbers and make phone calls, calling the desk clerk at a hotel in the foreign country to inquire about available lodgings, making an excursion to a grocery store in the foreign country) and the like. The options for creating activities are limited only by the facilitators' imagination, but it is important to remember that coherence will be a key ensuring that the activities are authenticated by the learners.

The objective of the interwoven hierarchy of themes, sub-themes and learning activities is to encourage the learners to communicate with each other and the facilitators right from the start while being exposed to and gradually starting to use the linguistic patterns of the new language. The facilitators will speak the Ln with the learners from the beginning, while also using other (essentially corporeal) modes of communication. But the learners will start out being solely dependent on those other modes as they begin to learn the Ln, which they will, however, gradually incorporate into their efforts to communicate with the facilitators and the other class members. Just as children acquiring their mother tongue are not provided with a grammatical syllabus, but still manage to become highly competent native speakers, there is no need to create a strict grammatical syllabus for SLE courses either. Learning activities can easily be designed to encourage learners to focus on and become comfortable with communicating about relatively simple relationships, physical objects, the here-and-now and concrete actions. Activities focusing on events in the past or the future, or ones that are dependent on conditions would logically come later, as would abstract and more complex concepts.

Without any sort of training, caregivers manage to provide precisely this sort of scaffolding to children acquiring their native tongues. In effect, in both cases, the scaffolding process is a symbiotic one. It is surely obvious that a parent or older sibling is very unlikely to speak with very young interlocutors about quantum mechanics, literary theory or tree diagrams from transformational grammar. By the same token, the SLE facilitator begins by introducing simple, palpable concepts and structures, leaving abstract and complex concepts for a later day, once the adult learner's communicative competence has emerged to a degree that would make such topics accessible to them in the Ln. Of course the adult learner is capable of thinking about and even discussing complex, abstract topics in their native tongue and perhaps other languages as well. But the monolingual SLE environment is designed to retrace the same kind of trajectory in terms of cognitive complexity that the native speaker child experiences. The results of our courses demonstrate that this approach functions very well indeed, and at a speed far surpassing that of the most precocious native speaker infant.

From this perspective, there is clearly a fine line the facilitator will need to walk between 'teaching' particular linguistic forms and 'exposing' learners to grammatical structures that they can perceive and extrapolate themselves from communication. The distinction between affordances and input is essential in this context. It is important to remember that from the perspective of the *Natural Approach*, 'comprehensible input' is received passively and is all but automatically incorporated into an internal representation or facsimile of a language. From the perspective of SLE, each learner personally generates (albeit through communication with others) his or her own language through a proactive, creative and embodied process.

When creating and introducing learning activities, it is essential for facilitators to keep in mind the importance of the perceived authenticity of the activity for the learners. The latter need to engage themselves in the proposed learning activities and see them as opportunities for undertaking genuine communication whenever possible. It is good to avoid terms like 'exercises' or even 'games' when talking about learning activities as exercises are reminiscent of conventional 'teaching' activities (that are not likely to be authenticated (accepted as authentic) by the learners, and games may be considered childish and not worthy of serious involvement. Learning activities can and should often be fun, but there is usually a certain degree of seriousness purpose involved in them that encourages learners to authenticate them as full-fledged learning opportunities.

Promoting peer collaboration

Adopting Vygotsky's view that cognitive development is dependent on and in fact derives from collaborative communicative interaction, it is essential from the SLE perspective that most learning activities have a significant collaborative component. Instead of trying to 'teach' the students separately and individually, facilitators should put them in authenticated situations in which they have little choice but to work together and hence communicate with each other. This provides fertile ground for language emergence. Instead of investing large amounts of time and energy into lesson plans involving the transmission of knowledge about the Ln to the individual students, facilitators will find themselves investing time and energy into creating interesting, stimulating and relatively open-ended collaborative activities (all within the thematic themes discussed above) for the learners to engage in: activities that promote communication but that exclude the native tongue, and that hence foster Ln emergence. The range of activities developed by our SLE student-facilitators is vast and continues to grow, course after course, particularly because we have no textbook or list of required pre-defined activities. Each team creates almost all of its own activities, essentially from scratch.

A few collaborative activities, however, have proven to be almost universally applicable and effective and have been passed on from one group of facilitators to the others. A good example is the labyrinth activity, in which students move in pairs through a labyrinth made with tables and chairs in the classroom. One partner is blindfolded and the other is not. Each sighted learner gives instructions to his or her blindfolded partner, for example: "take three steps forward", "turn left", "stop", "reach up with your left hand", etc. The guiding learners may not touch their blindfolded partners and hence must use the Ln to give instructions. The objectives include having the guides produce comprehensible and appropriate instructions so that that their partners complete their navigational task without bumping into the furniture, and having the blindfolded partners be required to decipher and negotiate the instructions given to them by their partners. Activities of this type also promote autonomy in learners, providing them with the self-confidence that comes from communicative success within the context of a (minimally) risky authenticated task. The labyrinth also provides opportunities to actually work with the comprehension and production of instruction in general and to use the corresponding linguistic structures in an embodied context. Rarely does a good learning activity serve just one purpose. It is up to the facilitators to design them in such a way as to expand and maximize a variety of positive effects for the learners and their emergent Ln.

Fostering embodied learning: involving the body in the learning process

It may require a special effort for new facilitators to include a corporeal component in almost all of their SLE learning activities, as conventional language classes often involve an active teacher but passive learners. A good way for both facilitators and learners to begin to rediscover the natural links between mind and body is to take advantage of the *Total Physical Response* (TPR) technique on a regular basis throughout an intensive SLE course and beyond. Some forms of instruction, particularly involving basic linguistic operations can play a key role in SLE courses for students with no prior knowledge of the Ln. We have found variants of TPR to be extremely valuable techniques for introducing individual words – the basic building blocks of emergence for any Ln. In our SLE courses at the FTSK, it is common for facilitators to include at least one TPR activity for the introduction of new terminology every day. Each activity will clearly be directly related to the sub-theme for that day (and by extension to the overall theme chosen for the course). Adult learners can thus start out by being introduced to a broad panoply of simple terms (designations for everyday objects and simple physical actions) and then moving on to words that can modify those designations, all the while without resorting to the crutch of word-for-word translation. Bodily actions, gestures and facial expressions will accompany this instructional process through TPR, allowing learners to bootstrap themselves within a matter of days into the one- and then the two-word stages of Ln production, which the infant would require many months to achieve. Grammaticalisation, the natural process of identifying and incorporating linguistic patterns in the Ln, builds upon the incipient knowledge of this body of lexical items.

It is important to focus first on the spoken language which is communicated through (and/or accompanied by) prosodic features, facial expressions, proxemics and body language. If the written language is set aside for at least the first week of an SLE course, learners will learn to resort to using multiple senses to perceive meaning, just as they did when they acquired their native tongue. Particularly when the written form of the Ln uses the same writing system as the learners' native tongue or other languages they know, learners tend to resort only to their sense of sight in order to perceive the language. We have also found in working with 13 languages in intensive SLE courses that learners tend to achieve excellent pronunciation very quickly, apparently because they are confronted for a number of hours per day with the aural form of the new language enunciated by their native-speaker facilitators in authenticated contexts.

It is of course essential to have space in the classroom for moving around. A conventional classroom, often filled to the brim with rows of chairs facing the teacher's desk in the front of the room, simply must give way to a less linear classroom layout in which learners and facilitators are free to move. As it is assumed that SLE courses will most often be offered in an intensive format, it should not require an inordinate amount of time and effort to modify the environment to make it more amenable to holistic learning that includes a major corporeal element. In our courses, we most often remove most of the tables and chairs from a large classroom, retaining just enough chairs for the learners to use to form a large circle or islands for small-group work. We choose carpeted classrooms whenever possible to improve the acoustics in the room and also to make the environment cosier and to permit learners to sit on the floor if the occasion arises. The stark walls of a conventional classroom offer themselves as the perfect blank support for drawings and photographs, texts produced by the learners, and realia from the Ln culture. We have found that decorating the room is an excellent way to foster authentication, or perceived authenticity of the learning environment.

Welcoming complexity into the language learning classroom

> *"The world bubbles forth."* – Heraclitus

One of the most striking things I have noticed when coaching new SLE facilitators is the difficulty that many have in truly sharing authority and control in the classroom. They often feel the need to plan every aspect of every activity from start to finish and to take responsibility, not only for learning, but for everything that goes on in the classroom. This is, of course, not surprising as we have all spent a good portion of our lives in conventional classrooms where the teacher, lecturer or instructor by default assumes responsible for the content of instruction, the sequencing of the accumulation of knowledge, and all of the actions and activities that occur in the classroom. After all, the teacher is considered to be the one with the knowledge of the language that learners wish to acquire and it is logical in this context for the provider of knowledge and skills to maintain control over the process of transferring them to the learners.

The SLE classroom, on the other hand, is understood as a complex, non-linear, self-creating and self-maintaining microcosm of a social world – one in which the respective L:n plays a key but unbalanced role – it has already emerged in the facilitators but is only about to begin emerging in the learners. To be successful using this approach, facilitators need to see their role in terms of initiating communication, facilitating the bootstrapping language emergence within the learners and guiding each unique learner along his or her respective path towards embodying that new language. They need to set aside the idea that they are trying to teach, instruct or transmit knowledge of the language or skill in using it to learners. Facilitators need not and should not plan out every minute of what is to happen in the classroom. Instead, they should offer opportunities for authenticated social interaction to occur in the classroom environment; interaction that they may initiate but that will take its course as a function of the myriad dynamic features of the classroom context at every moment. Complexity cannot be scripted and it cannot be controlled. But it is the complex social, cognitive, emotional and corporeal interaction with a language that allows its very emergence within learners.

Closing words and an invitation

Some 2,700 years ago, the ancient Greek thinker Heraclitus reportedly said not only that we cannot step into the same river twice but also that: "The world bubbles forth". His was an ancient view that today is embodied in the understanding of our world in terms of non-linear complexity. Complexity Thinking suggests that this perspective can be useful not only for conceptualising such things as the genesis of the universe from a pinpoint to a still expanding sky-filling vastness. It can also help us understand the nature of the emergence into the world of utterly unique human beings after a brief gestation period – each one of them having started out as single cell just nine months before. And even in the foreign language learning realm, I suggest, complexity thinking can help us see that a language can "bubble forth" – emerge – from the immeasurably complex, utterly unique and eminently dynamic interplay of forces of nature and nurture. This is a process that cannot be predicted or controlled. But it is my conviction that facilitators can and do participate in the bootstrapping and scaffolding of language emergence.

Considerable space has been devoted in this volume to methods and approaches that I have worked with and learned from, and that date back decades; I owe a tremendous debt to all of them and to those who developed and proposed them – even those with whom I disagree today. Innovation in language learning and teaching have always been the result, I believe, of dialogue and debate, borrowing and recasting, theorising and practical pedagogy in ever-evolving educational and classroom settings. There can be no single, best way to teach foreign languages; there can only be more or less pragmatically useful ones for a given time and even each given group of learners. I have found the SLE approach to be particularly useful in our FTSK environment and our motivated and already successful language students. It will be up to other would-be facilitators and educational researchers to determine whether this particular approach can be useful elsewhere and perhaps for other types of students.

I hope that some of my readers will be tempted by the prospect of experimenting with this approach in the classroom, and that some will be moved to empirically investigate the abductively generated claims on which it is based. Is there still room for yet another 'alternative' approach to language teaching? My experience with SLE suggests to me and to many who have learned with this approach that there is. I am hopeful that the experiences and theoretical considerations presented here will engender dialogue with others interested in non-transmissionist foreign language learning.

References

ARNOLD, J. (1999): *Affect in Language Learning*. Cambridge, UK: Cambridge University Press.

ASHER, J. (1977): *Learning Another Language Through Actions: The Complete Teacher's Guidebook*. Los Gatos, California: Sky Oaks Publications.

ATKINSON, D. (2011): *Alternative Approaches to Second Language Acquisition*. Abingdon & New York: Routledge.

ATKINSON, D. (2011b): "A sociocognitive approach to second language acquisition", in: ATKINSON, D. (Ed). *Alternative Approaches to Second Language Acquisition*. Abingdon & New York: Routledge, 143–166.

BLEYHL, W. (2005): "Die Definite des traditionellen Fremdsprachenunterrichts oder: Weshalb ein Paradigmenwechsel, eine Umkehr in der Fremdsprachenunterricht erfolgen muss", in: *Fremdsprachen lehren und lernen* 34, 45–64.

BROWN, J. S.; COLLINS, A.; DUGUID, S. (1989): "Situated cognition and the culture of learning", in *Educational Researcher* 18 (1), 32–42.

BRUNER, J. (1960): *The Process of Education*. Cambridge & London: Harvard University Press.

BRUNER, J. (1978): "The role of dialogue in language acquisition", in A. SINCLAIR; R. J. JARVELLE, & W. J.M. LEVELT (eds.): *The Child's Concept of Language*. New York: Springer-Verlag.

BUCKLEY, FRANCIS J. (2000): *Team Teaching: What, Why and How?* Thousand Oaks: Sage Publications

CROUSE, D. (2012): "Going for 90% plus: How to stay in the target language", in *The Language Educator* 7 (5), 22–27.

DALKE, A. F.; CASSIDY, J.K.; GROBSTEIN, P.; BLANK, D. (2007): "Emergent pedagogy: learning to enjoy the uncontrollable and make it productive", in: *Journal of Educational Change* 8, 111–130.

DAVIS, B.; SUMARA, D. (2006): *Complexity and Education: Inquiries into Learning, Teaching and Research*. Mahwah, N.J: Lawrence Earlbaum.

DAVIS, BRENT; SUMARA, DAVIS (2008): "Complexity as a Theory of Education", in: *Transnational Curriculum Inquiry* 5(2), http://nitainat.library.ubc.ca/ojs/index.php/tci, 33–44.

DAVIS, BRENT & SUMARA, DENNIS (2010): "If things were simple ...: complexity in education", in: *Journal of Evaluation in Clinical Practice*, 16 (4) 856–860.

DAVIS, B.; STIMMT, E. (2003): "Understanding learning systems: mathematics teaching and complexity science", in: *Journal for Research in Mathematics Education* 34(2): 137-167.

DICKINSON, L.; LEVEQUE, J.; SAGOT, M. (1975): *All's Well 1: Teacher's Book*. Paris: Marcel Didier.

DICKINSON, A.: LEVEQUE, J.; SAGOT, L. (1975): *All's Well That Starts Well*, Paris: Didier.

DIEKHOFF, J.S. (1965): *NDEA and Modern Foreign Languages*. N.Y.: Modern Languages Association of America.

DOLL, W. E. (1993): *A Post-Modern Perspective on Curriculum*. New York: Teachers College Press.

DUNN, W. E.; LANTOLF, J.P. (1998): "Vygotsky's Zone of Proximal Development and Krashen's $i+1$: Incommensurable Constructs; Incommensurable Theories", in: *Language Learning* 41/3, 411-442.

ELLIS, N. (1998): "Emergentism, connectionism and language learning", in: *Language Learning* 48 (4), 631-664.

ELLIS, N. ; O'DONNEL, M. & RÖMER, U. (2015): "Usage-based language learning", in: MCWHINNEY, B. & O'GRADY, W. (eds.): *The Handbook of Language Emergence*, Chichester: John Wiley Sons, 163-180.

FINCH, A. (2001): "Complexity in the classroom", in: *Secondary Education Research*, 47, 105-40.

FERRO, T. R. (1993): "The influence of affective processing in education and training", in: *New Directions for Adult and Continuing Education* 59, 25-33.

FILIPOVIC, Z.; FILIPOVIC, R.; WEBSTER, L. (1972): *English by the Audio-Visual Method*. Paris: Didier.

FINCH, A. (2004): "Complexity and systems theory: Implications for the EFL Teacher/Researcher", in: *The Journal of Asian TEFL* 1(2), 27-46.

FROESE, VICTOR (Ed.) (1991): *Whole Language Practice and Theory*. Boston: Allyn & Bacon.

GIBSON, JAMES J. (1979): *The Ecological Approach to Visual Perception*. Hillsdale NJ: Erlbaum.

GOODMAN, N. (1978): *Ways of Worldmaking*. Indianapolis: Hackett Publishing Co.

GREGG, K. (1984): "Krashen's monitor and Occam's razor", in: *Applied Linguistics* 5, 79-100.

HOPPER, P. (1987): "Emergent Grammar", in: *Proceedings of the Thirteenth Annual Meeting of the Berkeley Linguistics Society*, 139-157

KARIMI-AGHDAM, S. (2016): "A dialectical reading of Dynamic Systems Theory: Transcending socialized cognition and cognized social dualism in L2 studies", in: *Language and Sociocultural Theory* 3 (1), 55–82.

KIRALY, Don (2000): *A Social Constructivist Approach to Translator Education*, Manchester: St. Jerome.

KIRALY, DON (2014): "Förderung autopoietischer Fremdsprachenbildung – von der holistischen Sprachbegegnung zur autonomen Aneignung von fortgeschrittenen fremdsprachlichen Fertigkeiten", in: GUTENBERG LEHRKOLLEG DER JOHANNES GUTENBERG-UNIVERSITAT: MAINZ (eds.) *Gute Lehre – von der idee zur Realitat Innovative Lehrprojekte an der JGU*. Bielefeld: Universitatsverlag Webler, 121–134.

KIRALY, DON (2015): "Language acquisition in the classroom: from tasks to enaction", in: KRINGS, H.P. & KUEHN, B. (eds.): Fremdsprachliche Lernprozesse: Erträge des 4. Bremer Symposiums zum autonomen Fremdsprachenlernen. Bochum: AKS Verlag.

KRASHEN, S. (1982): *Principles and Practice in Second Language Acquisition*. Upper Saddle River, NY: Prentice Hall.

KRASHEN, S. & TERRELL, T. (1983): T*he Natural Approach: Language Acquisition in the Classroom*. Oxford: Alemany Press.

KUMARAVADIVELU, B. (2003): *Beyond methods: Macro-strategies for Language Teaching*. New Haven, CT: Yale, University Press.

LAKOFF, G. & JOHNSON, M. (1999): *Philosophy in the Flesh: The Embodied Mind and its Challenge to Western Thought*. New York: Basic Books.

LARSEN-FREEMAN, D. (1997): "Chaos/complexity science and second language acquisition", in: *Applied Linguistics*, 18 (2), 141–165.

LARSEN-FREEMAN, D. & CAMERON, L. (2008): *Complex Systems and Applied Linguistics*, Oxford: Oxford University Press.

LARSEN-FREEMAN, D. (2011): "A Complexity Theory Approach to Second Language Development/Acquisition, in ATKINSON, D. (ed.): *Alternative Approaches to Second Language Acquisition*, Abingdon & New York, 48–72.

LARSEN-FREEMAN, D. (2007): "On the complementarity of chaos/complexity theory and dynamic systems theory in understanding the second language acquisition process", in: *Bilingualism: Language and Cognition*, 10 (1), 35–37.

LIU, D. (2015): "A Critical Review of Krashen's Input Hypothesis: Three Major Arguments", in: *Journal of Education and Human Development*, 4 (4), 139–146

MACARO, E. (2001): "Analysing student teachers' codeswitching in foreign language classrooms: Theories and decision making", in: *Modern Language Journal*, 85 (4), 531–548.

MCLAUGHLIN, B. (1987): *Theories of second-language learning*. London: Edward Arnold.

MACWHINNEY, B. & O'GRADY, W. (2015): *Handbook of Language Emergence*. Malden, MA: Wiley-Blackwell.

MEDDINGS, L. & THORNBURY, S. (2009): *Teaching Unplugged: Dogme in English Language Teaching*. Surrey: Delta Publishing

MORÇÖL, G. (2001): "What is Complexity Science? Postmodernist or Postpositivist?" in: *Emergence*, 3 (1), 104–119.

NEWELL, C. (2008): "The class as a learning entity (complex adaptive system): An idea from complexity science and educational research", in: *SFU Educational Review*, 2 (1), 5–17.

NORMAN, D. (2008): "Signifiers – not affordances", in: *Interactions*, Nov.–Dec., 18–19.

PARADIS, MICHEL (2009): *Declarative and Procedural Determinants of Second languages*. Amsterdam: John Benjamins.

RICHARDS, J.C. & RODGERS, T.S. (2014): *Approaches and Methods in Language Teaching*. Cambridge University Press: Cambridge.

RICHARDSON, K. & CILLIERS, P. (2001): "What is Complexity Science? A View from Different Directions", in: *Emergence* 3 (1), 5–23.

RISKU, H. (2010): "A Cognitive Scientific View on Technical Communication and Translation. Do embodiment and situatedness really make a difference?, in: *Target* 22 (1), 94–111.

RUTHERFORD, W. E. (1987): "The meaning of grammatical consciousness-raising," in: *World Englishes* 6 (3), 209–216

STEVICK, E. W. (1980): *Teaching Languages, A Way and Ways*. Boston: Heinle & Heinle Publishers.

SMITH, B. (ed.) (1988): *Foundations of Gestalt Theory*, Munich and Vienna: Philosophia Verlag.

SUMARA, D. & DAVIS B. (1997): "Enactivist theory and community learning: toward a complexified understanding of action research", in: *Educational Action Research* 5 (3), 403–422.

TAYLOR, J. R. (2004): "Some pedagogical implications of cognitive linguistics", in: GEIGER, R.A. & RUDZKA-OSTYN, B. (eds.): *Conceptualisations and Mental Processing in Language*, De Gruyter, 201–226.

TOMASELLO, M. (2011): "Language development", in: USA GOSWANI (ed.): *Wiley-Blackwell Handbook of Childhood Cognitive Development*, Chichester: Blackwell Publishing Ltd, 239–255.

UNDERHILL, A. (1999): "Facilitation in language teaching", in: ARNOLD, J. (ed.): *Affect in Language Learning*, Cambridge, UK: Cambridge University Press.

VAN LIER, L. (1996): *Interaction in the Language Curriculum: Awareness, Autonomy, and Authenticity*. London: Longman.

VAN LIER, L. (2000): "From input to affordance: social-interactive learning from an ecological perspective", in: LANTOLF, J.P. (ed.): *Socio-cultural Theory and Second Language Learning*. Oxford: Oxford University Press, 245–259.

VAN LIER, L. (2005): *The ecology and semiotics of language learning: a sociocultural perspective*. Boston: Kluwer Academic Publishers.

VARELA, F. J.; THOMPSON, E. & ROSCH, E. (1991): *The Embodied Mind: Cognitive Science and Human Experience*. Cambridge: MIT Press.

VARELA, F.; MATURANA, H. & URIBE, R. (1974): "Autopoiesis: the organization of living systems, its characterization and a model", in: *Biosystems* 5, 187–195.

VYGOTSKY, L. (1994): "Extracts from Thought and Language and Mind in Society", in: B. STIERER & J. MAYBIN (eds.): *Language, Literacy and Learning in Educational Practice*. Clevedon, UK, 45–58

WESCHE, M. B. (2002): "Early French Immersion: How has the original Canadian model stood the test of time?", in: BURMEISTER, P.; PISKE, T. & ROHDE, A. (Eds.): *An integrated View of Language Development. Papers in Honor of Henning Wode*, Wissenschaftlicher Verlag, Trier, 2002, 357–379.

WHITEHEAD, A.N. (1950): *The Aims of Education and Other Essays*. London: E. Benn.

Unpublished BA and MA Theses Cited

BURING, MARIE: "Holistic Second Language Acquisition in the Classroom – A Fresh Look. A Case Study at the FTSK: A Naturalistic Introduction to the Russian Language". Masters thesis, University of Mainz, 2014.

DESTREEL, JOERI: "Language emergence: Developing and teaching a Dutch language course for beginners". Masters thesis, University of Mainz, 2017.

HEINRICHSOHN, SABINE: "Second Language Acquisition – Naturalistic Approach". Bachelors thesis, University of Mainz, 2015.

NAGI, JENNIFER: "The Natural Approach within the Framework of the CEFR in a Case Study of a Hungarian Course". Postgraduate thesis, University of Mainz, 2010.

RIZZO, ALESSIA: "The Naturalistic Approach: From Theory to Praxis. The Ongoing Process of Designing an Italian for Beginners Course at the FTSK". Bachelors thesis, University of Mainz, 2015.

SCHEU, STEFANIE JANINE: "Towards Improving Second Language Instruction in the Refugee Classroom: A Case Study". Masters thesis, University of Mainz, 2016.

WITTNER, ANNIKA: "A Qualitative Case Study on the Teaching Competence of Undergraduate Students of the FTSK". Bachelors thesis, University of Mainz 2013.

SPRACHEN LEHREN – SPRACHEN LERNEN

Bd. 1   Martina Nied Curcio/Peggy Katelhön/Ivana Bašić (Hg.): Sprachmittlun g – Mediation – Mediazione linguistica. Ein deutsch-italienischer Dialog. 326 Seiten. ISBN 978-3-7329-0094-7

Bd. 2   Claudio Di Meola/Joachim Gerdes/Livia Tonelli (Hg.): Grammatik im fremdsprachlichen Deutschunterricht. Linguistische und didaktische Überlegungen zu Übungsgrammatiken. 316 Seiten. ISBN 978-3-7329-0268-2

Bd. 3   Tiberio Snaidero: Interkulturelles Lernen im Italienischunterricht. Eine Konzeption und Lernaufgaben für Italienisch als 3. Fremdsprache. 436 Seiten. ISBN 978-3-7329-0331-3

Bd. 4   Donald Kiraly & Sarah Signer: Scaffolded Language Emergence in the Classroom. From Theory to Practice. 144 Seiten. ISBN 978-3-7329-0259-0

Bd. 5   Milica Sabo: Universalkonzepte im Fremdsprachenunterricht. Eine qualitative Studie zu sprachenübergreifenden Lehr-Lernprinzipien. 304 Seiten mit CD. ISBN 978-3-7329-0382-5

Bd. 6   Martina Nied Curcio/Diego Cortés Velásquez (Hg.): Strategien im Kontext des mehrsprachigen und lebenslangen Lernens. 320 Seiten. ISBN 978-3-7329-0451-8

Bd. 7   Beate Baumann: Sprach- und kulturreflexives Lernen in Deutsch als Fremdsprache. 272 Seiten. ISBN 978-3-7329-0430-3

Bd. 8   Claudio Di Meola/Joachim Gerdes/Livia Tonelli (Hg.): Germanistische Linguistik und DaF-Didaktik. 242 Seiten. ISBN 978-3-7329-0463-1

Bd. 9   Martina Nied Curcio/Peggy Katelhön: Sprachmittlung und Mediation für Deutsch als Fremd- und Zweitsprache (DaF/DaZ). 228 Seiten. ISBN 978-3-7329-0630-7

Bd. 10 Isabella Matticchio/Luca Melchior (Hg.): Mehrsprachigkeit am Arbeitsplatz. 198 Seiten. ISBN 978-3-7329-0644-4

Frank & Timme

SPRACHEN LEHREN – SPRACHEN LERNEN

Bd. 11   Naima Tahiri/Mohammed Laasri/Said El Mtouni/Rachid Jai-Mansouri (Hg.): Germanistik und DaF in mehrsprachigen Kontexten. Sprachdidaktische, interkulturelle und systemorientierte Perspektiven. 238 Seiten. ISBN 978-3-7329-0650-5

Bd. 12   Peggy Katelhön/Pavla Marečková (Hg.): Sprachmittlung und Mediation im Fremdsprachenunterricht an Schule und Universität. 252 Seiten. ISBN 978-3-7329-0745-8

Bd. 13   Katja Abels/Silvia Hansen-Schirra/Katharina Oster/Moritz J. Schaeffer/Sarah Signer/Marcus Wiedmann (eds.): Re-Thinking Translator Education. In Honour of Don Kiraly's Social Constructivist Approach. 324 Seiten. ISBN 978-3-7329-0827-1

Außerhalb der Reihe erschienen ist:

Peggy Katelhön/Martina Nied Curcio: Hand- und Übungsbuch zur Sprachmittlung Italienisch – Deutsch. 288 Seiten. ISBN 978-3-86596-425-0

F Frank & Timme